Successfully Managing ADHD

Behaviour issues in general, and ADHD in particular, is always a high priority in schools. Teachers are constantly searching for practical guidance on how to manage learners who find it difficult to concentrate and stay on task for any length of time, sometimes presenting challenging behaviour in the classroom and disrupting learning for other students.

Fintan O'Regan provides a user-friendly resource for busy teachers, showing them how to offer practical and effective strategies and models of good practice to practitioners, and signposting further sources of information. Chapters in this essential book cover topics such as:

- How can we manage ADHD behaviour?
- How can we help non-traditional learners access the curriculum?
- Working with parents of children with ADHD
- Making transitions less problematic
- Exploring other options for managing ADHD
- The role of medication and how/when it can help.

Written by one of the UK's leading experts on the topic, SENCOs, teachers, behaviour management staff and senior leaders will find invaluable, practical and up-to-date information and advice on ADHD and will be able to use the resources provided as a continuing professional development tool with colleagues in all phases.

Fintan O'Regan is currently an International Behaviour and Learning Consultant and an associate lecturer for Leicester University, the National Association of Special Needs and the Institute of Education. He is also the Vice Chairman of UK ADHD Partnership, a member of the European ADHD Alliance and former chairperson of the European ADHD Taskforce.

nasen is a professional membership association that supports all those who work with or care for children and young people with special and additional educational needs. Members include teachers, teaching assistants, support workers, other educationalists, students and parents.

nasen supports its members through policy documents, journals, its magazine Special!, publications, professional development courses, regional networks and newsletters. Its website contains more current information such as responses to government consultations. nasen's published documents are held in very high regard both in the UK and internationally.

Other titles published in association with the National Association for Special Educational Needs (nasen):

Brilliant Ideas for Using ICT in the Inclusive Classroom
Sally McKeown and Angela McGlashon
2011/pb: 978-0-415-67254-2

Language for Learning in the Secondary School
A Practical Guide for Supporting Students with Speech, Language and Communication Needs
Sue Hayden and Emma Jordan
2012/pb: 978-0-415-61975-2

Assessing Children with Specific Learning Difficulties
A Teacher's Practical Guide
Gavin Reid, Gad Elbeheri and John Everatt
2012/pb: 978-0-415-67027-2

Using Playful Practice to Communicate with Special Children
Margaret Corke
2012/pb: 978-0-415-68767-6

The Equality Act for Educational Professionals
A simple guide to disability and inclusion in schools
Geraldine Hills
2012/pb: 978-0-415-68768-3

More Trouble with Maths
A teacher's complete guide to identifying and diagnosing mathematical difficulties
Steve Chinn
2012/pb: 978-0-415-67013-5

Dyslexia and Inclusion
Classroom approaches for assessment, teaching and learning, second edition
Gavin Reid
2012/pb: 978-0-415-60758-2

Provision Mapping
Improving outcomes in primary schools
Anne Massey
2012/pb: 978-0-415-53030-9

Beating Bureaucracy in Special Educational Needs
Helping SENCOs maintain a work/life balance, second edition
Jean Gross
2012/pb: 978-0-415-53374-4

Promoting and Delivering School-to-School Support for Special Educational Needs
A practical guide for SENCOs
Rita Cheminais
2013/pb: 978-0-415-63370-3

Time to Talk
Implementing outstanding practice in speech, language and communication
Jean Gross
2013/pb: 978-0-415-63334-5

Successfully Managing ADHD

A handbook for SENCOs and teachers

Fintan O'Regan

Routledge
Taylor & Francis Group

LONDON AND NEW YORK

First published 2014
by Routledge
2 Park Square, Milton Park, Abingdon, Oxon OX14 4RN

and by Routledge
711 Third Avenue, New York, NY 10017

Routledge is an imprint of the Taylor & Francis Group, an informa business

British Library Cataloguing in Publication Data
A catalogue record for this book is available from the British Library

Library of Congress Cataloging in Publication Data
O'Regan, Fintan J. (Fintan Joseph), 1960–.
   Successfully managing ADHD: a handbook for SENCOS and teachers/
   Authored Fintan O'Regan. – First edition.
   1. Attention-deficit-disordered children – Education – Great Britain –
   Handbooks, manuals, etc.   2. Special education – Great Britain –
   Handbooks, manuals, etc.   I. Title.
   LC4713.5.G7O75 2014
   371.9 – dc23
   2013038036

ISBN: 978-0-415-74857-5 (hbk)
ISBN: 978-0-415-59770-8 (pbk)
ISBN: 978-1-315-81392-9 (ebk)

Typeset in Sabon and Gill Sans
by Florence Production Ltd, Stoodleigh, Devon, UK

Contents

Foreword

Lorraine Peterson

This latest book from Fintan O'Regan on ADHD offers a comprehensive and practical guide for all those working with children and young people in schools, especially SENCOs and teachers.

There has always been a conflict between the fact that ADHD is a medical condition and covered by the National Institute of Clinical Excellence (NICE) and the need for educational support and guidance to ensure that all these children and young people have their needs met in Early Years settings, schools and colleges. The latest NICE guidelines have highlighted that ADHD is a life-long condition so, if there is no 'cure', schools need to understand how to manage ADHD behaviours effectively and support individuals in their quest for a happy and fulfilling life – both within the education system and in the world at large.

The author has tried to answer many of the common questions and address the key issues about the ADHD condition, while also providing the reader with the most current information on the topic.

The book is easy to read and laid out in an accessible format so that it will meet the needs of those who are starting to explore the topic because their professional judgement is telling them that a child they are teaching is exhibiting challenging behaviours whilst at the same time supporting those professionals working with children and young people diagnosed with ADHD and offering them support and guidance in meeting their needs within their educational setting.

The new SEN Code of Practice, which will become statutory guidance from September 2014, is very clear that the majority of children and young people with identified SEN will have their needs met through mainstream provision. This will include many of those with ADHD. If all teachers are responsible for the progress and development of the pupils in their class then we need to ensure that all teachers have the knowledge and skills to both identify need and offer strategies and interventions to ensure that every pupil can access education alongside their peers.

The Code of Practice also introduces a new category of need; social, mental and emotional health needs replacing behaviour, social and emotional needs. This is to try and concentrate on the primary needs of individuals and not put all the emphasis on the behaviour. Teachers working with pupils with ADHD and associated behaviours will need a deeper understanding of the condition and how best to support the children and young people they are teaching. This book will address this.

This book provides a wealth of practical guidance, support and information that can be used for individual or whole school professional development to ensure a better understanding of ADHD and associated behaviours. It is being published at a time of radical SEN reform and offers all educational settings timely advice on the topic of ADHD and I recommend that every school has a copy to support their workforce in impacting on the educational opportunities for all children and young people especially those with ADHD or associated behaviours.

Acknowledgements

This book is for all the dedicated SENCOs, teachers and teaching assistants who every day change the lives of so many children and young people suffering with ADHD.

Introduction

Attention Deficit Hyperactivity Disorder (ADHD) is one of the most researched, discussed and written about conditions in the world today and yet it remains a highly controversial subject. Though a significant number of children, adolescents and adults are living with the reality of ADHD, many people are still in doubt about the existence of such a 'condition'.

During my work over the last 25 years as both a head teacher and behaviour and learning consultant, I have had to answer many questions regarding ADHD. I have also listened to many opinions and points of view regarding this subject, many of which run along the lines of, '*ADHD is just an excuse for bad behaviour*'.

My responses to this kind of challenge have varied, but have tended to go something like . . . '*ADHD is not a psychological problem or just an excuse for difficult behaviour. It's a biological condition that occurs when the brain is not quite as finely tuned as it needs to be*'.

As a result of hearing so many teachers voicing these doubts however, I decided to write a book that would try to answer many of the common questions and issues about the ADHD condition, while also providing the reader with the most current information on the topic. Another reason for a new book is that ADHD is no longer seen solely as a childhood issue: National Institute of Clinical Excellence (NICE) guidelines have highlighted that ADHD is a life-long condition or as one observer put it, '*if you are born with it, you die with it*'. If there is no 'cure', we surely need to understand how to manage ADHD behaviours effectively and support individuals in their quest for a happy and fulfilling life – both within the education system and in the world at large.

Two recent headlines caught my eye:

Primary School fails in High Court bid to overturn ruling on ADHD exclusion

and

Too special to queue? ADHD children get theme park pass.

Why does the term 'ADHD' command so many controversial headlines and arguments? Other SEN terms such as Dyslexia, Dyspraxia, Aspergers and Bi-polar Disorder if not immune to criticism, seldom appear to feature in the same way. It appears to me, that despite national and international recognition, many parents and professionals appear confused and even suspicious about the term 'ADHD' itself and this gets in the way of them considering the best options of management. This can't be helpful – to either the 'doubters' or to the individuals in question.

This book will attempt to provide some clarity and confidence in both understanding and managing individuals who are impulsive, inattentive and often hyperactive within the school setting. I am an educator rather than a doctor or physiologist, and have tried to give practical suggestions for teachers wherever possible.

There are some difficult and controversial issues to be explored, for example the use of medication, the relevance of equality or disability discrimination legislation and the numbers of exclusions affecting children with ADHD. There can be no finite answers to many of the questions surrounding these topics, but knowledge and understanding will lead readers to better informed and reasoned (if still subjective) opinions.

Who should read this book?

Anyone who knows children or adults with ADHD will find this book useful, but it has been written with SENCOs, behaviour management staff and senior leaders specifically in mind. They are the people tasked with informing colleagues about pupils' additional/special educational needs and providing appropriate continuing professional development (CPD). One of their main responsibilities is to equip teachers to manage such children and young people effectively, remove barriers to learning and ensure 'enjoyment and achievement'. I have tried to provide readers with the tools to help colleagues develop a greater understanding of the issues surrounding ADHD, as well as providing a range of strategies that may enable successful and proactive intervention.

Behaviour issues in general (whether or not attributable to ADHD) are always a high priority in schools. Teachers are constantly searching for practical guidance on how to manage learners who find it difficult to concentrate and stay on task for any length of time; who sometimes present challenging behaviour in the classroom and disrupt learning for other students. In this book, you will find a user-friendly resource that enables you to offer practical and effective strategies and models of good practice to colleagues. Key points from each chapter are summarized and can be used in CPD sessions (Chapter 10). There are also some 'true or false' statements to use with colleagues as a starting point for discussion, enabling the presenter to dispel some myths about ADHD and begin to establish a shared understanding amongst staff. In this way, schools can build an ethos of tolerance and inclusion, where learners who have difficulties with paying attention and conforming to behavioural norms, can be managed effectively and enabled to succeed.

In summary, the book:

- provides practical guidance and off-the-shelf material for delivering CPD to staff, ensuring a better understanding of ADHD and associated behaviours and the impact they have on children and their families
- offers practical tips on achievable, proven approaches and models of good practice in the classroom and beyond, including interventions and ways of using support staff
- explains the new NICE guidelines and legal requirements for the administration of medication for ADHD which you need to know about
- includes guidance on working with parents. SEN legislation encapsulated in the Children and Families Bill (2013/14) places an emphasis on schools clarifying their support for children and young people with SEN, explaining this to parents and involving them more in the decision making process
- encapsulates all relevant issues raised by teaching pupils (of any age) with ADHD in an up-to-date, well-informed and accessible way.

One final point to make which I think is very important and will be a recurring theme of this book is that, in my opinion there is no such thing as an 'ADHD child' or an 'ADHD adult', but there are some children and adults who have ADHD. This is an important difference and fundamental to how well we can maximise the long-term prospects of the individuals concerned.

Chapter 1

Why is the issue of ADHD so important?

One of the questions often asked is: '*Why do we appear to have an explosion of ADHD cases in UK schools?*' Part of the answer is a growing awareness and understanding of the condition by people from all sectors of society. In common with other categories of special educational needs, ADHD has become a much more familiar term in recent years as it has escaped the confines of medical and psychological realms and entered into the consciousness of educators and the general public.

But there is a marked reluctance amongst UK professionals to copy what is regarded as 'over reaction' to this condition of child behaviour (for example, by countries such as the USA). This results in some of our children who have ADHD remaining unidentified and 'untreated'. Parents are all too often having to fight for recognition that ADHD is a real condition, and having to argue for the resources and services to support their children.

> ADHD has become a much more familiar term in recent years as it has escaped the confines of medical and psychological realms and entered into the consciousness of educators and the general public

As greater awareness and understanding of the condition develops amongst a range of professionals, this situation should improve. There is a pressing need for the classification and diagnosis of ADHD in the UK to be seen within a multi-agency context. This will mean that professionals from health, education and social services come to a shared agreement about what it is, and what can be done to help people who experience difficulties because of the condition.

Research

A research report conducted across health professionals in the UK in 2006 ('ADHD: Paying enough attention?') raised three key issues:

1. There are barriers to diagnosis and treatment
2. ADHD is under-diagnosed
3. If undiagnosed and untreated, ADHD has a significant impact on a person's life.

A survey of child and adolescent psychiatrists and paediatricians in the UK had informed the report. The majority of respondents (54%) thought that ADHD was under-diagnosed in the UK, and that fellow professionals in health and education lacked understanding of the condition (see BOX 1).

The Key Recommendations for the future included the following points:

• Teachers need increased education, resources and support in order to improve their approaches to children with ADHD, and to provide advice to parents about how to access the healthcare system

---

BOX 1 Survey of psychiatrists and paediatricians

Amongst those health professionals who responded to the survey:

- 54% stated ADHD is under-diagnosed in the UK
- 43% specialists stated that teachers were not aware of ADHD so don't realise children should be referred
- 54% of specialists felt GPs are unsure of which patients to refer
- 90% felt ADHD can lead to difficulties in finding a job and keeping a job
- 97% stated that children with under-diagnosed ADHD are more likely to drop out of school
- 85% said that not treating childhood ADHD can lead to adult mental health problems such as depression and even suicide
- 98% of specialists stated that behavioural therapy together with pharmacotherapy is the most effective for treating ADHD, yet only 34% use this for their patients

---

- GPs should receive education about ADHD in order to improve diagnosis and levels of appropriate referral for secondary care
- Secondary care needs additional specialists to ensure that the waiting time is shortened for a first referral and patients can be seen more often
- Patients should have access to the most effective management strategy; currently this does not happen, due in part to parental concerns regarding medication
- There needs to be a greater understanding of ADHD amongst the general public and the media in order to remove the fear of being branded or blamed as a failure
- There needs to be increased information for parents to increase their understanding and ensure they seek help from their GP.

It is interesting to consider how far we have moved on since these recommendations were made – if at all. Certainly, there remains a great deal of scepticism, particularly amongst a number of GPs, that ADHD is a genuine condition and not an environmental issue of poor parenting. This is despite the guidance from NICE whose recommendations on ADHD in 2008 were as follows:

- ADHD is a real and genuine condition
- A range of measures including educational and behavioural strategies can improve the outcomes of children with ADHD
- Medication can and should be used to improve the outcomes of individuals who suffer with ADHD symptoms
- Adult services should recognise the need to monitor and treat individuals with ADHD and continue to treat individuals previously under CAMHS when necessary.

A steadily improving awareness and understanding of diverse needs and acceptance of an ethos of 'equal rights' will hopefully bring about changes in attitude to how we identify and provide for children and young people with ADHD, within an inclusive and multi-agency approach.

A shared understanding and ethos

Is ADHD an excuse or an explanation for inattentive, hyperactive and impulsive behaviour? Is it used as a 'smoke screen' for badly behaved children by incompetent parents who provide too many carbonated drinks, an inappropriate diet and fail to ration time spent on video and computer games?

This continues to be the debate in many schools, not just in the UK, but across the globe. Whether or not these factors contribute in any way, the established fact is that many children are exhibiting behaviours that will affect not just their own opportunities and success levels, but the opportunities, achievement and well-being of the children and teachers around them. Family life at home can also be seriously affected. Within schools, professional development and good leadership and management is central to establishing a shared understanding of the issues surrounding ADHD and appropriate ways of supporting the children and young people affected.

> Is ADHD an excuse or an explanation for inattentive, hyperactive and impulsive behaviour? Is it used as a 'smoke screen' for badly behaved children by incompetent parents who provide too many carbonated drinks, an inappropriate diet and fail to ration time spent on video and computer games?

Everyone involved in education needs to understand that ADHD affects all aspects of a child's life. In Chapter 2 we look in more detail at how the condition manifests itself in different ways, but there are some basic tenets to be established within a shared ethos:

- Children with ADHD are often distractible and demanding and, if not managed effectively, can also be defiant, disruptive and possibility even dangerous
- ADHD can hinder a child's communication and interaction with other people, it can stop him or her from learning facts and skills essential for success in life, and it can cause behavioural, emotional and social difficulties which affect his or her psychological well-being
- In spite of their difficulties, children and young people with ADHD can be highly creative and positive learners, excelling in some areas.

Some facts and figures

In school, the impact of ADHD on both the child and other children can be difficult to manage successfully and in some cases there are negative outcomes. In an ADDISS (Attention Deficit Disorder Information and Support Service) survey of over 500 parents of children with ADHD, 39% reported that their child had been excluded from school for a 'fixed term' as a result of their condition, with 11% having been excluded permanently (ADDISS 2006). Anecdotal evidence suggests that more recent figures do not show any significant improvement.

ADHD persists into adolescence and adulthood in a significant proportion of people. In a recent survey, 90% of health professionals agreed that having ADHD can lead to difficulties in finding a job (see Box 1). Furthermore, people with ADHD are at higher risk of antisocial behaviour; substance misuse disorders and substance misuse; criminal activity and imprisonment (Waslick and Greenhill 2005).

To illustrate this further, data collated by the Youth Justice Board shows that a high percentage of young offenders are considered to be impulsive and to act without thinking, clearly showing linkage to the key symptoms of ADHD. It seems that these individuals act without premeditation. One experienced police officer commented: *'the first time they think about it, it's too late – they have already done it'*.

> A steadily improving awareness and understanding of diverse needs and acceptance of an ethos of 'equal rights' will hopefully bring about changes in attitude to how we identify and provide for children and young people with ADHD, within an inclusive and multi-agency approach

People with ADHD can continue to find socialisation difficult and are more likely to have relationship problems and suffer from social isolation than people without the condition. A reported 50–70% are more likely to have few

> ADHD can hinder a child's communication and interaction with other people, it can stop them from learning facts and skills essential for success in life, and it can cause behavioural, emotional and social difficulties which affect their psychological well-being

or no friends (Cooper and O'Regan 2001). This group is 40% more likely to experience teenage pregnancy and 20–30% more likely to experience depression (Intl Consensus 2002).

Research has shown that children with ADHD can be very unhappy at school. The following quotes are taken from the *Parent and Child Research Document* produced by the national Parent ADHD advocacy group, ADDISS, in 2006:

> 'I get picked on every day, I got picked on today, and I got picked on yesterday. Every single day. They make names up and they always do it when there aren't any teachers around. If they knew, they wouldn't be able to do anything about it. I just get treated weird. Like an Alien.'

'I just wish I didn't have it. I'd do anything not to have it. It ruins your life.'

Parental views

The views of parents and their concerns about the treatment of children with ADHD are regularly reported by ADDISS. The time taken for diagnosis of the condition is a continuing source of frustration. Whilst the process can take less than 6 months, many families have reported that, for them, the route to diagnosis took between 1 and 5 years, thereby placing their children at an extreme disadvantage.

Some other findings of an ADDISS conference for parents included:

- 75% of children with ADHD received medication
- For 1 in 6 of these children, medication started before the age of six
- Diagnosis of ADHD is usually made by a consultant in psychiatry, psychology or paediatrics
- Very few consultants provide details of a support group, yet more than half of parents reported that a support group had been of most value to them
- Social Services were repeatedly regarded as the most unhelpful group. Most respondents said that professionals in this sector didn't recognise ADHD as a disability and rarely offered support for respite care
- Parents agreed that training of teachers in handling children with ADHD was vital yet only a minority found that teachers in their child's school received specific training in ADHD
- 50% of children with ADHD had a Statement of Special Educational Needs providing a range of support in school (it will be interesting to note how this compares with the proportion of children afforded an Education, Health and Care Plan under the new SEN system).

> People with ADHD can continue to find socialisation difficult and are more likely to have relationship problems and suffer from social isolation, than people without the condition. A reported 50–70% are more likely to have few or no friends

Finally the parents were asked to say what had made the most difference to them and their family, of which the majority said: '*Getting a diagnosis and treatment*'.

However members of one family were quite clear when they said '*it was the teacher of Year 3 Class*' (in a school in Suffolk) who had made all the difference to their child.

A summary of key points that parents felt would make the biggest difference to their children is provided as a handout on page 74 in Chapter 10 and would make a useful starting point for some CPD with colleagues. **The overwhelming need expressed by parents is for better training on ADHD for teachers.**

In summary then, the issue of ADHD is important because if children with this condition are not recognised and given appropriate help and support, their learning will be impeded, possibly resulting in underachievement. The accompanying frustration and low self-esteem may have a negative impact on all aspects of their lives – and the lives of people around them.

Chapter 2

When is it ADHD?

ADHD is a developmental disorder characterised by significant deficits in inhibiting behaviour (self-control), sustaining attention to tasks, resisting distractions while doing so and controlling one's activity level to meet the demands of a situation. The hyperactive and impulsive symptoms appear to comprise a single underlying problem with behavioural inhibition, which is often the first problem to be seen.

What is the prevalence of ADHD?

It is estimated that ADHD affects up to 5% of all children, making it the most common behavioural disorder in the UK (Cooper & O'Regan 2001). The disorder often runs in families, develops in childhood, often by 3 to 5 years of age, if not sooner, and is highly persistent across development in most, though not all, cases. Most experts agree, children diagnosed in childhood continue to be impaired by the disorder in adolescence, and that a majority continue to have symptoms producing impairment into adulthood.

> It is estimated that ADHD affects up to 5% of all children, making it the most common behavioural disorder in the UK

What are the symptoms of ADHD?

As outlined above, lack of focus, poor control, impulsivity, inappropriate behaviours and distractibility are often hallmarks of children who are diagnosed with ADHD. The symptoms, however, are not necessarily seen to the same degree in all children diagnosed. As a result, clinicians recognise three subtypes of the disorder:

- the hyperactive–impulsive type
- the inattentive type
- the 'combined' type, when both appear together (this describes the majority of cases).

(The recently revised DSM-5 (2013) now describes three presentations, see BOX 2a below.)

It is often children within the Hyperactive Impulsive Type or Combined Type who are noticed within the school community as they exhibit such demanding symptoms. However, it is also very important to consider the Inattentive Type child (sometimes categorised as having 'attention deficit disorder' or ADD) who are much easier to overlook. Recent research is now suggesting that the inattentive type may actually comprise an entirely separate, distinct disorder where the primary features are poorly focused attention, 'hypoactivity' (less than normal) and sluggish information-processing.

These children may appear withdrawn and listless and are often lonely and without friends. They can be spotted amongst the quiet pupils who seldom speak out or put up their hands to ask or answer questions. Such children (often girls) appear lost in their own thoughts, and may be regarded as 'dreamy' individuals; they often prefer their own company rather than wanting to join in group activities, discussions or games. They may seem unusually distracted, untidy or late with assignments and are frequently accused of not listening. These inattentive pupils do not attract attention by being demanding or disruptive, so it can be easy to assume that they are 'all right'; their lack of active engagement may significantly impair learning outcomes however, and lead to underachievement if the situation is not addressed.

> Recent research is now suggesting that the inattentive type may actually comprise an entirely separate, distinct disorder where the primary features are poorly focused attention, 'hypoactivity' (less than normal) and sluggish information-processing

Girls and ADD

There is a growing concensus that ADD is more prevalent in girls but they are less likely to be identified as having attention deficit than boys, especially when they are natural 'teacher-pleasers' and avoid drawing attention to themselves. Sadly, many girls with ADD (ADHD) never receive diagnosis and much-needed treatment. Many professionals believe that girls are less impacted by ADD (ADHD), and are unaware of the very real risks for them of chronic demoralisation, anxiety, depression, underachievement, teen pregnancy, cigarette addiction and substance abuse.

The good news is that ADD (ADHD) is a highly treatable condition. The earlier a girl receives the help and support that she needs, the more likely she is to function well at home, with her friends and at school, allowing her to live up to her potential.

Symptoms of ADD will overlap with the symptoms of low self-esteem: in both areas there are low energy levels, disorganisation, social withdrawal and trouble with concentrating. Even more confusing, the unrecognised ADD can lead to major coping problems, which in turn lead to actual depression on top of the ADD. This most often occurs at adolescence (although it can happen earlier). Doctors tend to zoom in on the diagnosis of 'depression' or 'anxiety disorder', rather than identifying ADD. (See Appendix 2 for an easy to use ADD checklist.)

Some of the signs that a girl has ADD may include:

- not feeling liked and accepted by other girls
- worries that they can't keep up with all that is expected of them
- fears that their teacher will become angry at them
- dread that they will be embarrassed in class
- a sense of being pummelled by criticisms and corrections every day.

> Their lack of active engagement may significantly impair learning outcomes, and lead to underachievement

For girls, disorganisation and distraction can result in:

- a lack of activity; they are too confused to get things started. Both genders have trouble learning the nuances of social interactions but too often, girls end up shy and withdrawn. They don't like the negative reactions they get when they don't clue-in to the nuances. Boys are more likely to proceed with social behaviour that is considered inappropriate; even if they get negative reactions, they continue
- an environment that is extremely disorganised: their lockers, bedrooms, school bags – even their handwriting, is a mess! Both genders have problems in this area but girls are expected to be 'good organisers', for themselves and others, whereas boys are more likely to get this done for them, when they can't do it on their own
- the demands of secondary school becoming too much: they may become tired and disheartened by poor school performance. The girls with hyperactivity may throw themselves into social

relationships to compensate, being described as 'boy-crazy' or 'party girls'. Girls with ADD/ADHD may begin to show more risky sexual behaviours and are more likely to use drugs or alcohol than youngsters who do not have the disorder and its accompanying low self-esteem. Shoplifting, teen pregnancy and eating disorders are also found more often in females with ADD.

BOX 2a The specific symptoms of different types of ADHD

Inattentive

- Pays little attention to detail in schoolwork or other activities; makes careless mistakes.
- Frequently has problems in sustaining attention (e.g. staying focused in lessons, or reading a lengthy text).
- Often seems not to be listening when spoken to directly.
- Often does not follow instructions and fails to finish tasks.
- Has difficulty with organising tasks and achieving good time management.
- Avoids and dislikes tasks which demand sustained mental effort.
- Constantly loses things.
- Is easily distracted.
- Often forgetful.

Hyperactive-impulsive

- Squirms and fidgets in seat; often restless.
- Often out of seat when staying seated is required.
- Often runs around or climbs excessively in situations where this is inappropriate.
- Has difficulty playing quietly.
- Constantly 'on the go'.
- Talks excessively.
- Blurts out answers before the questions have been completed.
- Often has difficulty with turn-taking.
- Frequently interrupts or intrudes on others' conversations or games.
- Tends to act without thinking.
- Is often impatient.
- Is uncomfortable doing things slowly and systematically.
- Finds it difficult to resist temptation.

The same primary symptoms for ADHD that are used as in DSM-IV are used in the DSM-5 to diagnose ADHD. They continue to be divided into two major symptom domains: Inattention and hyperactivity/impulsivity. And, like in the DSM-IV, at least six symptoms in one domain are required for an ADHD diagnosis.

However, several changes have been made in DSM-5 to the ADHD category, according to the APA:

- Examples have been added to the criterion items to facilitate application across the life span.
- The cross-situational requirement has been strengthened to 'several' symptoms in each setting.
- The onset criterion has been changed from 'symptoms that caused impairment were present before age 7 years' to 'several inattentive or hyperactive-impulsive symptoms were present prior to age 12'.
- Subtypes have been replaced with presentation specifiers that map directly to the prior subtypes.
- A co-morbid diagnosis with autism spectrum disorder is now allowed.
- A symptom threshold change has been made for adults, to reflect their substantial evidence of clinically significant ADHD impairment. For an adult diagnosis to be made, the patient only needs to meet five symptoms – instead of six required for younger persons – in either of the two major domains: inattention and hyperactivity/impulsivity.

What causes ADHD?

Like all developmental disabilities, such as learning disorders and intellectual disability, ADHD appears to have multiple causal components. Evidence suggests that neurological, genetic and environmental factors contribute to the condition.

Neurological factors

A number of research studies by world renowned expert Russell Barkley have suggested that parts of the brain (frontal and parietal lobes and part of the mid-brain) are not performing as well as they should in children with ADHD. Communication between the frontal lobes, which is responsible for executive function, and the parietal lobes, where action is initiated, may be slower to mature than in those children not affected. It is interesting to note that in DSM-5, ADHD has been moved to the section on neuro-developmental disorders, indicating that impairments extend beyond 'behavioural issues' and should be seen more as 'developmental learning difficulties'.

Genetic factors

ADHD is among the most genetically influenced (inherited) psychological disorders, with genetic factors explaining the severity of the symptoms among individuals. For instance, if there is one child with ADHD in a family, there is a 25–35% chance that another sibling may also have the disorder, and a 45% chance or greater that at least one parent has the disorder. If that child is an identical twin, the odds are that the second twin will have the disorder in 75% to 92% of cases (Faraone and Doyle 2001). Scientists are now searching for the genes that contribute to this disorder.

Pre-natal and birth factors

In a small percentage of cases, the disorder seems to arise as a consequence of developmental injury to these same brain regions, such as that due to maternal consumption of alcohol or tobacco during pregnancy, premature delivery with associated minor brain haemorrhage or accidental head injury after birth.

Environmental factors

Though neurological and genetic factors seem to be at the root of the disorder, environmental factors cannot be ignored as these may contribute to the manifestation of the behaviours that can be problematic. The evidence suggests that ADHD is unlikely to arise purely from social factors like poor parenting (child management), family stress, divorce, excessive TV viewing/video game-playing, or poor diet although some or all of these factors are likely to contribute to a child's difficulties.

An important consideration for teachers is how they can exercise control over environmental factors in school and implement useful interventions for children and young adults (more on this in Chapter 3).

How do you diagnose ADHD?

ADHD frequently occurs in combination with other issues, which makes diagnosis a complex process. No single professional can reach a valid diagnosis without the gathering of information from a range of sources and consideration of the contributions of key people in the child's life. Central to the process are the accounts of parents, teachers and, where appropriate, the individual concerned. The purpose is not only to arrive at diagnosis but also crucially, to identify the child's strengths, skills and talents. These will be the basis of successful interventions both in school and in other contexts. The emphasis should not be exclusively on 'problems'.

There is no one conclusive test of ADHD, but there is a range of tools that can build a picture of the student across a number of contexts and over extended timelines. The process of assessment for ADHD typically includes some or all of the following elements:

> There is a growing consensus that ADD is more prevalent in girls but they are less likely to be identified as having attention deficit than boys, especially when they are natural 'teacher-pleasers' and avoid drawing attention to themselves

- direct observation
- clinical interview
- behaviour checklists
- educational reports
- formal testing, paediatric and/or neurological investigation.

A first step in schools will often be referral to the SENCO by a concerned class teacher. A simple screening tool can be helpful at this stage and the Child ADHD Screening Tool (CAST) is provided in Appendix 1 to support SENCOs in the process of initial identification.

Direct observation

Real-life samples of the child's behaviour are most valuable and we know that many parents and teachers feel that seeing a child in the clinic only tells half the story. Psychologists and others will gain most by observing the child in as natural a setting as possible and if possible across a range of different settings to include home, school, outside play etc.

Clinical interview

A series of in-depth interviews must be undertaken with the child's parents or carers, yielding a detailed history of the child's birth, development, personality, relationships, functioning across a range of settings, and current problems. A less-structured interview is then held with the child or adolescent. This might involve different play activities and sometimes more structured tasks aimed at assessing concentration, attention, impulsivity and problem-solving, and cognitive style. Other significant people in the child's life may also be interviewed, including siblings, grandparents and childminders. These detailed interviews are regarded as the single most important part of the assessment because it is through these that the clinician can discern if a pervasive pattern of problems with inattention, impulsivity and hyperactivity are present or if the problems causing concern are due to other factors. The aim is to combine multiple perspectives to gain as clear a picture of the individual child or adolescent as possible.

Behavioural checklists

Several behavioural checklists or rating scales are routinely used to obtain reliable, valid and comparable accounts of the child or young person's behaviour. These standardised questionnaires are completed by key people, usually parents and teachers, and the student himself/herself.

Among the most commonly used are the Conners Parent and Teacher Rating Scales (1996a; 1997) which are available in both long and short forms. Factors identified by the teacher's version include:

> No single professional can reach a valid diagnosis without the gathering of information from a range of sources

- hyperactivity
- conduct problems
- emotional overindulgence
- asocial behaviour
- daydreaming and attentiveness.

The Conners scale helps to subtype and differentiate ADHD into the three main forms – Impulsive hyperactive, Inattentive or Combined. The Conners Abbreviated Symptom Questionnaire (1996) is a supplementary 10-item questionnaire which is typically used to measure the response to treatment interventions.

[Based on the same clinical expertise, research skills, and theoretical knowledge used to develop the scale for children and adolescents, the CAARS (Conners' Adult ADHD Rating Scales) has been designed to help assess, diagnose and monitor treatment of ADHD in adults. Two formats are included for self-report ratings and observer ratings. Both the self-report and observer forms provide multi-modal assessments of the same behaviours and problems, and contain an identical set of scales, subscales, and indexes. CAARS forms are available in long, short and screening versions. A new user's guide enables the instrument to be used effectively with correctional populations as well.]

Other instruments include the Achenbach Child Behaviour Checklist (1991), and the Home Situations and School Situations Questionnaires (Barkley 1981). The Achenbach is a wide-ranging assessment tool looking at a range of behaviours. It is considered the first step in the screening process to assess ADHD, and is generally followed up with a more ADHD-specific assessment tool.

Another recommended rating scale is the ADDES-2 (McCarney, 1995). It can be used to screen children aged 2 to 18 years and its main advantage is that it is linked to interventions presented in a cook-book type format. This is recommended if the user is looking for a scale linked directly to an intervention (Demaray et al. 2003).

Behaviour rating scales serve a critical function in the diagnosis of ADHD but should only be used as part of a multi-modal assessment (Power and Ikeda 1996). The context in which behaviour occurs is critical to the diagnosis.

The QbTest

The QbTest is a computer-based assessment that combines a test of attention ability with a movement analysis based on an infrared measurement system. Test results are assembled into a report and compared with norm data from other people of the same sex and age. This way the tester can compare reaction rates on a series of tasks in comparison with people who do not have ADHD.

The test is done in front of a computer screen. The test equipment consists of an infrared camera, a camera marker and a response button. During the test, a number of symbols are shown at regular intervals on the computer screen. The task of the participant is to push the responder button when the same symbol is repeated.

This is a common method for measuring attention and impulsivity, and at the same time the movement pattern will be recorded. The test is very easy to perform and can be completed in 15 minutes for children and 20 minutes for adolescents.

The QbTest is widely used in Europe and is being used in a growing number of UK centres. It is an objective tool that measures all three core signs of ADHD – inattention, impulsivity and hyperactivity in individuals between 6 and 55 years of age. It is not a conclusive test for ADHD but can be used together with other clinical information within a comprehensive assessment.

Educational reports

Both formal and informal reports should be sought and ideally the teacher or the year head should be consulted by the diagnosing professional. Information from the school is a critical part not only in the diagnosis itself, but also in terms of assessing the impact of the disorder on the child's educational experience and progress. Past school performance and behaviour are relevant too, not just the current situation. The type of information which teachers can provide includes assessment and evidence of the child's

- span of attention
- listening skills
- social behaviour

- work rate/completion
- on-task behaviour
- reaction to correction and instruction
- the level of organisation and planning
- memory
- level of aggression
- personality
- strengths and learning difficulties.

> The context in which behaviour occurs is critical to the diagnosis

In providing these data, teachers must be careful to be objective and to avoid exaggeration in an effort to support a possible diagnosis; exemplification is useful. Students should always be compared to their average peers, with the task, the context and the classroom demands in mind.

Formal testing; paediatric and/or neurological investigation

In the case of young children, a referral for paediatric medical investigation should also form part of the assessment, the purpose being to rule out the presence of any co-existing disorder which may complicate or account for the child's symptoms. Children are routinely checked for visual or hearing problems, for example. Where a child has other difficulties in addition to ADHD, these must be identified and treated in parallel. With older students and adults, a medical screening will also be essential especially where medication is considered as a component of any intervention.

BOX 2b Recognised diagnostic criteria

In order for a clinician to formally diagnose ADHD, there are a number of requirements to be met:

- the clinician must be able to note the presence of six or more of the symptoms (listed in BOX 2a) for either inattention or hyperactivity/impulsivity.
- these symptoms must have persisted for at least six months and be inconsistent with the child's developmental level.
- some significant degree of impairment must be present in two or more settings (e.g. home and school).
- some of the symptoms must have been present before the age of twelve.
- the symptoms should not be due to another disorder.
- there must be evidence of a significant level of impairment in social, academic or occupational functioning.

Adapted from the DSM-5 (American Psychiatric Association 2013).

Are there co-existing difficulties (co-morbidities)?

Many students with ADHD have other difficulties which affect their learning. When learning disorders are defined as resulting in 'performance significantly below the expected level', nearly 80% of students with ADHD meet this criterion while still in primary education (Cantwell and Baker 1992). However, when narrower definitions are used (such as academic achievement relative to intellectual functioning) the number drops to 2.5% or less (Barkley 1998b). Cognitive or intellectual deficits may underpin both the ADHD and the learning difficulties; in other children and adolescents, however, the ADHD and its associated conduct problems may be the main factors in the resulting poor academic performance.

Oppositional Defiant Disorder

Oppositional Defiant Disorder (ODD) is the term used to describe a certain pattern of behaviours that includes a child losing their temper frequently, defying adult authority, being easily annoyed and deliberately annoying others. The key elements displayed by children with ODD include the following characteristics:

- arguing with adults
- refusing to cooperate and defying instructions
- being angry and defensive
- being spiteful and vindictive.

In essence these children display a 'counter-will' against authority, especially when frustrated or stressed. They are often completely inflexible in these situations and the more pressure applied to make them conform, the greater their opposition. These are often the children who will say '*you can't make me*', '*it's not fair*' and '*get out of my face or I will sue you*'. (Gritting your teeth and holding back the urge to scream '*I will see you in court*', are to be advised!)

The reasons for and origins of this condition are difficult to detect, but often the pattern will indicate frustration and intolerance as a result of a range of issues. These could include learning needs such as Dyslexia, and behavioural needs such as unrecognised ADHD. Other reasons may be attachment problems in early stages of development, low achievement and associated low self-esteem, lack of structure or a combination of these factors.

> Children with ODD are into power and are extremely good at pushing emotional buttons as a result

Douglas Riley in his excellent book *The Defiant Child* (1999) describes children with ODD as living in a fantasy world where they can defeat all authority figures (see BOX 2c for other characteristics displayed by children with ODD). Children with ODD are into power and are extremely good at pushing emotional buttons as a result.

It is thought that over 5% of children have ODD and although in younger children it is more common in boys than girls, as they grow older, the rate appears to level out in males and females.

BOX 2c Behaviours of children with ODD (Oppositional Defiant Disorder)

- They build a fantasy in which they can defeat all authority figures
- They are optimistic and fail to learn from experience
- Their attitude is one of 'you must be fair to me no matter how I treat you'
- They seek revenge when angered
- They need to feel and be seen as 'tough'
- They believe that you (parents, teachers) will run out of moves eventually
- They feel equal to their parents
- They often emulate the behaviour of their least successful peers
- Their answers to most questions consist of 'I don't know'
- Their 'logic' revolves around denial of responsibility

ODD is diagnosed in the same way as many other psychiatric disorders in children and involves a multi-modal assessment including a review of the family and medical history.

Conduct Disorder

Conduct Disorder (CD) is a type of behavioural difficulty where pupils often bully and show aggression to others. The difference between students with CD and ADHD is mainly one of 'wilful intent'. A student with CD is more likely to be premeditated in his or her actions and have an alibi for every situation. In contrast, any thinking-through by the student with ADHD is often too late as he/she has already carried out the action.

The four key elements that describe Conduct Disorder are:

* aggression to people or animals
* destruction of property
* deceitfulness and/or theft
* serious violations of rules.

The causes of CD are uncertain as there are a myriad of factors to consider. An important issue in my opinion, is that of role models: children with CD often lack good role models and take their lead from inappropriate models of behaviour. It is more common for males with CD to continue on into adulthood with these types of problems than females, who more often end up having mood and anxiety disorders as they mature. Substance abuse is very high amongst youngsters in this group: 50–70% of ten year olds with Conduct Disorder will be abusing substances four years later (Disney et al 1991).

Consistent inconsistency

Children and young people with ADHD are characterised by 'consistent inconsistency'. Some days they can produce great work unassisted and within the allotted time, at other times, they struggle to stay on task and even with close supervision may not accomplish much. Their erratic performance perplexes teachers and parents and can create the impression of laziness. Barkley (2006) explains,

> 'The problem here is not that they cannot do the work, but that they cannot maintain this persistent pattern of work productivity the way others can.'

It is not entirely clear why those with ADHD show this striking pattern of inconsistency in their behaviour and productivity, however it is likely to be due to the core impairment of impulse control. Consistent levels of productivity involve the ability to inhibit the impulse to engage in other activities, so the more limited and erratic impulse control is, the more variable the pupil's performance will be (Barkley 2000). It follows then, that 'executive functioning', which involves planning, controlling and regulating one's activity is impaired as a result of the core difficulties associated with ADHD, and these students may have significant difficulties with self-management or self-regulation.

Hyper focus

It is important to remember that children, adolescents and even adults with ADHD are not always inattentive or easily distracted; they are also capable of focusing very intently on things that hold a particular interest for them. They can get so absorbed that they are oblivious to the world around them and the passage of time, spending hours playing a computer game or surfing the net. This hyper focus, like distractibility, is thought to be related to a dopamine deficiency in the brain's frontal lobes which play a role in regulating attention. Both distractibility and hyper focus represent problems in the regulation of the attention system in ADHD (Barkley 2008).

Students with ADHD can also find it hard to 'shift gears'. They will tend to persist in behaviours or activities they enjoy long after others would have moved on to other things and it would appear that they are drawn to things that give instant feedback. If it can be harnessed, this ability to hyper focus can be an asset. Some youngsters with ADHD are able to channel their focus on something productive, such as a particular school project. For others, the chance to focus on a preferred topic or activity can be used as a motivator or as a reward for completing a less interesting but important task (Kohlberg and Nadeau 2002).

> Children and young people with ADHD are characterised by 'consistent inconsistency'. Some days they can produce great work unassisted and within the allotted time, at other times, they struggle

Sleep disorders

ADHD is linked with a variety of sleep problems. For example a recent study found that children with ADHD had higher rates of daytime sleepiness than children without ADHD. Another study found that 50% of children with ADHD had signs of sleep disordered breathing, compared to only 22% of children without ADHD. Research also suggests that restless legs syndrome and periodic leg movement syndrome are also common in children with ADHD.

It is thought that sleep problems may be experienced by children either as a direct symptom of ADHD or an accompanying disorder, or as a result of stimulant medication; it is also possible, of course, that a child may experience sleep problems in the long or short term just as anyone else might – totally unrelated to ADHD. When comparing children with ADHD (not being treated with medication) to children without ADHD, most studies show no difference in total sleep time or the time it takes to fall asleep. There are a few trends that emerge, however, suggesting that children with ADHD

- show increased restlessness and periodic limb movements during sleep
- experience less rapid eye movement (REM) during sleep
- show a higher occurrence of parasomnias, nightmares and bedwetting.

Unfortunately, more study is needed before we fully understand these relationships. The use of medication may add another level of complexity to the issue. Parents of children treated with stimulants perceive a higher prevalence of sleep problems (29% versus 10% (The National Sleep Foundation 2013)), and this is most commonly insomnia. These effects are especially noted when doses are too close to bedtime.

Lack of restorative sleep can obviously lead to tiredness during the school day and exacerbate a child's difficulties with concentrating in class. It is important that teachers are made aware of this in relation to particular pupils.

In summary, we can say that ADHD is not as easy to diagnose as one may think. This is probably part of the issue of teachers not recognising it as a real condition: they have seen cases of children labelled 'ADHD' who actually are not.

When a child presents with significant difficulties as listed in Box 2a (The specific symptoms of different types of ADHD) on p.10, the teacher or SENCO should refer him/her to an educational psychologist for an assessment.

Chapter 3

How can we manage ADHD behaviour?

Children with ADHD can be successfully managed in mainstream schools and it seems that there are two main components of effective provision. The first of these may appear quite straightforward and simple: basically, if a student with ADHD is interested in the task he/she is set and achieving success with it, he/she is less likely to be distracted or disruptive. Obviously, it is impossible to create a specific curriculum that will be 'interesting all of the time' to the extent that it prevents students who are highly distractible and/or impulsive and hyperactive being bored on some occasions. But teachers need to ask themselves if they are doing enough to interest and motivate their learners. Are tasks matched to ability in a way that will challenge the student and take forward his/her learning? Is there variety in subject matter, teacher exposition, task, pace and acknowledgement? Are appropriate allowances made for the difficulties experienced by students in formal classroom settings? (I have considered these matters in Chapter 4.)

The other issue is whether the incentive for completing the task, and the sanction for not doing it, are meaningful to the child and effective in achieving compliance. This is the issue I will address in this chapter.

Rules

The evident inability to follow rules is, of course, one of the major complaints of teachers who work with students with ADHD. Understanding *why* they appear to disregard the rules will be the key to implementing strategies to deal with this issue.

> The behaviour of a child with ADHD can be frustrating and annoying. But it's crucial for teachers to remember that he/she is not doing it on purpose; although there is no obvious physical disability, ADHD is a genuine medical condition

The primary goal in teaching rule-governed behaviour to students with ADHD will be initially to identify clear guidelines addressing basic health and safety issues. They must also understand that there are areas of 'no compromise' such as physical and verbal abuse, failure to wear correct uniform and poor timekeeping.

Other important class and school rules should be as specific as possible and teachers should be encouraged to use multiple prompts to establish each rule, providing immediate feedback on the outcome. Re-enforcement of the rules will be achieved with consistent use of positive (and negative where appropriate) logical consequences.

Key rules should be devised in order of priority, such as the example given below (for secondary students).

- no physical or verbal aggression to others
- completion of written work and practical tasks
- use of mobile phones limited as set out in school policy
- no eating, chewing or drinking in class

- punctual timekeeping
- adherence to uniform or dress-code if there is one.

In positive terms, these could be presented as:

- Be polite at all times: avoid using any verbal or physical aggression
- Be conscientious: complete tasks on time, to the best of your ability
- Keep mobile phones in lockers during lesson time
- Keep drinks and snacks for breaktime: do not bring chewing gum to school
- Be punctual; arrive for lessons on time and complete homework by the hand-in date
- Be clean and smart: follow the school uniform code.

These are the six key rules that in my opinion, all students including those with ADHD should observe and I would suggest little or no compromise on the above issues, especially verbal or physical aggression. If a child cannot or will not try to avoid physically or verbally assaulting another pupil or staff member, then that child may lose his or her right to be in that class. Where some flexibility could exist is with less-serious issues of calling out, fooling about, fidgeting and poor organizational skills. Also keep in mind that the child with ADHD can get easily frustrated: stress, pressure and fatigue can break down the child's self control and lead to contravention of rules.

Rules should be devised by following a staged process involving the following:

- Stage 1: Agree on the rules with the students, and establish consequences and rewards
- Stage 2: Gain a commitment from parents/carers
- Stage 3: Review and reconsider the rules on a regular basis.

Priorities

If we accept the core symptoms of ADHD, then it is possible to argue that students affected are not rule breakers but just unable to filter out the demands of environmental stimuli, all of which will be priorities for their attention. Traditional learners can and will ignore a chair being scraped behind them while the teacher is talking to them; the child with ADHD will turn to check out who is making the noise without thinking of the reaction of the teacher (unless the subject or task being discussed has a particular interest for him/her). In the mind of a child with ADHD, everything is equally important to attend to, and so the first principle will be to train him/her to prioritise where to focus his/her attention at any given time.

To some extent, the initial task may be to help children with ADHD beat the distractions that take their attention away from the rules of engagement. This is not an impossible task but it is going to take time. One way of starting the process is for a child to make a list of which distractions generally interfere with concentration and task completion in order to identify which areas will be of regular concern.

> Is the incentive for completing a task, and the sanction for not doing it, meaningful to the child and effective in achieving compliance?

This can be powerful on two fronts: first, it provides a clear and relatively straightforward focus for intervention and, secondly, it affords the child or adolescent a responsible role in helping to address obstacles to his/her learning.

From here it may be possible for the teacher to work with the child to prevent specific interference e.g. by changing seating arrangements, closing a window or pulling down a blind. Alternatively, the learner can be provided with some form of concentrator to manipulate, or allowed to doodle when the teacher is talking: in practice, this allows him/her by 'fiddling' to focus more effectively.

Rewarding success

Success breeds success, or so the saying goes. Students with ADHD are more likely to comply or be hooked into task completion and behavioural targets if they get a positive response to their efforts. If rewards are to work effectively as an incentive however, they must be allocated often and immediately, for realistic and measurable targets.

Verbal and non-verbal praise is the most accessible and frequently-used incentive in classrooms. Experienced teachers are adept at using praise but perhaps it may be useful to remind ourselves (and colleagues) from time to time of the important features of positive feedback (see BOX 3a).

Though praise itself can be a powerful tool, concrete evidence of teacher satisfaction will be vital in providing feedback that is sufficiently effective with children who have ADHD. The most effective method for instant and tangible feedback is through stickers and target charts which communicate very clearly that the child has met the expectations outlined. It is not my intention here to patronise teachers and learning support staff by writing about the management of positive reinforcement; but it is important to remember that stickers and stars should only be awarded if the child has met a creditable target. If stickers are allocated too generously, the child will quickly come to realise this and their value will be diminished.

> If rewards are to be an incentive, they must be allocated often and immediately, for realistic and tangible targets

Target charts

Children with ADHD will need any number of re-enforcers and it may well be an effective strategy to develop a specific positive recording system regarding particular behaviours or learning targets. Target charts would be an excellent means of acknowledging positive outcomes. It is suggested that these be used not instead of regular class reward systems such as team points, house points etc. but alongside as an additional motivator.

Points collected should be 'cashed in' for specific rewards, and regular, positive communication with parents and carers should take place to share the child's success. These charts can be issued at the beginning of the day/week/month as appropriate and can be either attached to student desks or remain with them as they move from class to class. They can cover break times and lunchtimes as well if non-structured time is a difficult part of the day for the child.

A sample chart is provided as BOX 3b. Such charts should be scored against specific targets and consistently managed and recorded (one or two points awarded). If the child has failed to meet the targets set or if a child is absent for the lesson then an X is put in the box. Bonus points could also be awarded for outstanding achievement either within the specific target issue, or another example of positive behaviour or learning outcomes.

Examples of rewards that the points could be cashed for include:

- certificates
- additional responsibilities in the class
- choice of activities (as part of lessons)
- free time
- ICT options
- informing parents of positive issues
- option of special area of interest i.e. Music, Art, Sports
- freedom of movement
- choice of work/class options
- field trips, outings
- lunch with teacher or headteacher (yep some kids like this!)
- reduced homework
- phone tokens, food, money or cash vouchers (for older students).

BOX 3a Key features of effective praise and positive feedback

Consistency

This seems obvious but we are all prone to different moods and different sets of circumstances. Behaviour that earns a positive comment one day may seem a 'minimum requirement' on another day unless there are clear benchmarks, targets and criteria. Pupils with ADHD may have a very strong sense of what is 'just', so consider how to achieve consistency:

- From day-to-day and lesson-to-lesson
- Between staff and support staff
- Between home and school
- Between pupils – differentiation in responding to individuals so that the well-behaved don't feel resentful when a child with ADHD gets praised to the skies for doing what they themselves do as a matter of course – all day, every day.
- Some secondary schools find that a marking template used across subject areas is effective in encouraging staff to clearly and quickly recognise effort, presentation and grading as well as areas for development.

Honesty

Children and young people are quick to spot insincerity so be sure that praise is properly deserved. Avoid using praise:

- to mollify a pupil who is being truculent
- for underachievement
- too 'gushingly', where everything is 'fabulous', 'excellent', 'terrific'; overuse renders these superlatives meaningless and leaves you nothing in reserve for when a child's achievement is truly outstanding.

Specificity

Vague expressions of praise such as 'good boy' and 'well done' are less effective than clear acknowledgements of specific behaviours. Build up a varied bank of phrases such as:

- 'I really like how you listened carefully to my instructions . . .'
- 'I'm very pleased that you sat patiently during that ten-minute session . . .'
- 'You did well to stick at that task and finish it before break – well done!'
- 'You're thinking much more carefully before answering questions . . . this shows me how sensible you can be.'
- In terms of assessment for learning feedback, make sure that comments are structured in a way that tells the pupil what went well (WWW) and how he/she could improve (even better if – EBI). For younger learners, the 'three stars and a wish' approach can work well.

Delivery

The age and personality of the child with ADHD will dictate how to deliver praise most effectively. Older pupils may not be pleased to receive overt praise in front of peers for example; for them, a quiet word during or after the lesson is more acceptable. Non-verbal acknowledgements may also be useful; a smile, a nod, a thumbs-up or a 'conspiratorial wink' may be powerful reinforcers when the relationship between teacher and pupil is sufficiently sound.

BOX 3b A sample target chart

	Day 1 Points X/1/2	Day 2 Points X/1/2	Day 3 Points X/1/2	Day 4 Points X/1/2	Day 5 Points X/1/2
Lesson 1					
Lesson 2					
Lesson 3					
Lesson 4					
Lesson 5					
Lesson 6					
Break					
Lunch					
Total					
Bonus					
Teacher sig					
Parent sig					

Student name_____ Start Date _____

Behavioural/Learning Target_____

Scoring:

2 = Great Job: Target behaviour/learning issue achieved
1 = Good Job: Target behaviour/learning issue achieved
X = Target not achieved or child is absent for the lesson

Overall, although the range of rewards above appears extensive and to some readers may seem extravagant, for example the possible use of money for older students, the principal element is that in most cases everybody 'has a price'. The key is trying to establish what that price is. For some primary aged students, feeding the fish or cleaning out the hamster cage is a major reward: for others, their position in the lunch queue might be an important incentive.

I am not suggesting schools or teachers 'pay' students to work or behave well, but if recognition of performance is recorded and communicated with parents and carers and this works for the child then it is an option worth looking at. The most important issue worth mentioning is that rewards should only be given consistently for tangible achievement. What works for one student however might not work for another and also what works one day might not work the next . . . finding reward systems that work consistently is a constantly developing process.

> Regular, positive communication with parents and carers should take place to share the child's success

Sanctions

The key element of using sanctions is to try to keep the sanction as private as possible and avoid humiliating the child in front of peers: we should resist the temptation to 'make an example of him/her'. This will not always be possible however, and in these cases teachers should try to appear to regret the action they have been forced to take, e.g. 'I'm afraid your actions leave me no choice . . .'. In addition, it is always useful to reaffirm the point that it will be the actions of the pupil that are being dealt with and not the pupil themselves, e.g. 'that was unacceptable behaviour' rather than 'you are a naughty boy'. Depersonalizing the situation is very important for all students but especially for students with ADHD.

It is also important to make clear the fact that the student has made a choice about complying or not complying and that the decision is their's. A scale of step-by-step sanctions, gradually increasing in severity if a student fails to comply with the initial request, is advised. The teacher (even if angry and frustrated) remains professional and appears cool on the outside. Sometimes, it may be useful to offer a 'suspended sanction' (a 'yellow card'), i.e. one that could be deactivated if the student complies for the remainder of a set period as determined by the teacher.

> As with rewards, the key with sanctions is consistent application in a business-like fashion.

Some options in the sanction list could be:

- displeasure of supervisor
- docking of points, merits etc.
- moving student to teacher's choice of seat
- restriction of free time at break/lunch
- time out
- informing parents of negative issues
- detention
- removal of privileges
- fines
- removal from a specific class for a fixed period
- removal from school for a fixed period.

As with rewards, the key with sanctions is consistent application in a business-like fashion. Hopefully, the child will register his/her actions as a mistake and will intend not to do the same again.

It is important for the sanction to be given as clearly and quickly as possible after the misdemeanour (although as mentioned above the sanction should be delivered if possible away from the group as 'public floggings' seldom pay dividends if remediation and not revenge is required).

Having said all of this, it is important to remember that what works well for some students works differently for others. Some students with ADHD respond very well to a sanction-loaded framework rather than a rewards process, and so the best advice is to tailor the approach to the specific child.

In addition to the above, the set of generalised behavioural intervention techniques listed in BOX 3c has proven helpful with students with ADHD.

Managing disruptions

One of the most difficult parts of managing students with ADHD is the issue of avoiding and dealing with disruptions in the classroom. One effective technique involves the use of non-verbal direction. Most direction by teachers is done through verbal instructions, but research has shown that non-verbal direction can be much more effective for children with ADHD.

BOX 3c General behaviour intervention strategies

- **Selectively ignore inappropriate behaviour.** This technique is particularly useful when the behaviour is unintentional or unlikely to recur, or is intended solely to gain the attention of teachers or classmates (without necessarily meaning to disrupt the classroom or interfere with the learning of others).
- **Remove nuisance items.** Teachers often find that certain objects (such as rubber bands and rulers) distract the attention of students with ADHD in the classroom. The removal of nuisance items is generally most effective after the student has been given the choice of putting it away immediately and then fails to do so.
- **Provide calming manipulatives.** While some items and other objects can be distracting for both the students with ADHD and peers in the classroom, some children can benefit from having access to objects that can be manipulated quietly. Manipulatives, or 'concentrators' may help children gain some needed sensory input while still attending to the lesson.
- **Allow for 'escape valve' outlets.** Permitting students with ADHD to leave class for a moment, perhaps on an errand (such as returning a book to the library), can be an effective means of settling them down and allowing them to return to the room ready to concentrate.
- **Activity reinforcement.** Students receive activity reinforcement when they are encouraged to perform a less desirable behaviour before a preferred one.
- **Hurdle helping.** Teachers can offer encouragement, support and assistance to prevent students from becoming frustrated with an assignment. This help can take many forms, from enlisting a peer or TA for support to supplying additional materials or information.
- **Parent conferences.** Parents have a critical role in the education of their offspring and this axiom may be particularly true for those with ADHD. As such, parents must be included as partners in planning for the student's success. Partnering with parents entails including parental input in behavioural intervention strategies, maintaining frequent communication between parents and teachers and collaborating in monitoring the student's progress.
- **Peer mediation.** Members of the peer group can positively impact the behaviour of students with ADHD. Formalised peer mediation programmes are effective options where specific students have received training in order to manage disputes involving their classmates.

General advice in terms of reducing disruption and improving attention is to use your own presence by moving near to the child on occasions that you think warrant this approach. Simply standing close behind or beside the child can often dampen the activity level of an individual to a dramatic effect without a word being spoken about the child's behaviour. Tactical ignoring of attention-seeking behaviour is another option, with 'a knowing look', or a shake of the head making it clear that this is not acceptable, can be enough. If only you or a few students appear affected by actions which are more covert, a quick tap on the shoulder and a word in the ear that you will catch up with them later may be enough.

If the actions are more disruptive and affecting the whole class, meet the situation with a firm but business-like approach saying that this behaviour is not appropriate. Give only one warning that if the behaviour is repeated there will be consequences. One warning, not two, is to be advised.

Finally, praise for appropriate responses will always be a welcome option. It's also worth considering involving the rest of the class in supporting children with ADHD. Encourage them to help by not 'winding them up' or provoking them into being the class clown.

Managing aggression

Verbal or physical aggression towards either peers or teachers warrants our full attention. Regardless of the causes, whether frustration at not learning, or other experiences of being misunderstood, aggression cannot be tolerated. Reversing aggression can take a great deal of time and supervision. In some cases, the issues are multi-faceted in origin and therefore will be multi-agency in management, involving some or all of the following: counsellors, peer mentors, form tutors, parents, social services, health professionals.

Aggression towards others by students with ADHD should result in logical consequences. A student who exhibits this trait on a regular basis has to be trained that aggression towards others will result in an immediate response from teachers, with no warnings necessary. The usual sanction is to remove the student from the classroom and place in a 'time out' zone or other suitable, stimuli-free area. There are a number of 'Time Out' systems but probably the best structured approach is the 1, 2, 3 Magic system by Thomas Phelan, a highly effective home and classroom behavioural modification system.

Further to this, the two techniques of overcorrection and positive practice should be utilised. For example, in the situation where a student loses control and throws a chair against the wall, breaking the chair in the process, the following should take place.

- the student goes to the time out area until in control
- the student pays for the replacement of the chair
- the student tidies all the chairs under the desks in that class at the end of the day for the next two weeks.

If this pattern of response seems unlikely, the school and its staff will need to take stock: without it, the child's aggressive tendencies may continue, and possibly escalate. '*Who has the time?*' I hear you say. Well, '*make the time*' is the only answer I can give you: time spent up front on this will save a lot more time and resources in the future.

Other options in dealing with aggression include teaching the child to use hesitation and calming techniques before the red mist gains momentum, and to find alternative ways of dealing with aggressive feelings and attitudes (more on this in Chapter 7).

> Parents have a critical role in the education of their offspring, and this axiom may be particularly true for those with ADHD. As such, parents must be included as partners in planning for the student's success

Teacher power

Although behaviour management may be about the use of clearly communicated systems and strategies, it also involves the ways in which specific teachers respond to certain situations. Teachers need to look at their own levels of performance, patience and, to some extent, relationships with pupils in order to reference how successful they will be in managing pupils with ADHD, who may be demanding, defiant and 'different'.

The issue of 'power' is all-important as it will be the success of how this teacher power is applied that will determine outcomes. Cooper and Olsen in their book *Dealing with Disruptive Students in the Classroom* outline teacher power in the following way:

1. Coercive power: based on punishment
2. Record power: praise/appraisal
3. Legitimate power: status of teacher or student
4. Referral power: liking/respect of teacher/pupil
5. Expert power: respect of knowledge.

These five bases of power are divided into two groups: 1, 2, and 3 are 'positional powers'; 4 and 5 are 'personal powers'.

All teachers have their own style within which they manage their classrooms and individual students based on their own personalities and their interpretation of how the rules should be adhered to and applied. As already mentioned, students with ADHD will often be engaged if they are interested in the subject, or attracted to the person who is managing them depending on the 'personal powers' listed above. It is for every individual teacher to assess which powers they wish to exert when working with particular pupils.

> Knowing some techniques for diffusing the situation and avoiding an escalation is an invaluable skill-set for teachers and other staff

It is often said that 75% of behaviour management should be by non-verbal means and due to the fact that ADHD students are often visual learners, this principle is worth thinking about. Although short, sharp, verbal redirection is often effective, non-verbal responses through eye contact, facial expression and gestures, use of hands and even physical proximity to students should be used when possible.

Having said this, verbal approaches that emphasise a positive 'you can do' approach can also be very beneficial. Many children with ADHD will have low self-esteem and will be expecting negative reactions, therefore it is a good idea to try to tell them what you want them to do, as opposed to 'what not to do'. It is always a good idea to say to a child '*I need you to*' rather than '*Can you . . .?*' or '*Will you . . .?*', as the latter requests are easier to say '*no*' to. '*I need you to*' is a more personal approach and more difficult to ignore or reject.

Other tips would be to think about the following:

*   Not to ask '*Why?*' ask '*What?*' e.g. '*What should you be doing now?*'
*   Use a three-word instruction that includes name, task, please . . . e.g. '*David, sit down, please*'.
*   Use, '*Stop*', '*Wait*', '*Think*' instead of '*No*'.
*   Use either/or and when/then, e.g. '*Lewis either put the phone in your bag or on my table*', '*when you have put the chair back under the table, then you can go*'.

Confrontations

It is useful for teachers to be aware of issues that in a heated situation might inflame a child's aggression. Understanding how to avoid these 'triggers' is an important part of behaviour management.

Issues likely to cause confrontations might include a teacher, other adult or peer:

*   bringing up past conflicts
*   not listening to the pupil's views or explanations
*   going 'face to face' (toe to toe)
*   raising his or her voice
*   finger pointing, teeth bearing.

Knowing some techniques for diffusing this kind of situation and avoiding an escalation is an invaluable skill-set for teachers and other staff. Diffuse confrontational behaviour by:

*   being calm but assertive
*   letting the student speak
*   using appropriate body language; palms of hands/hands by side
*   using time out options
*   trying to divert attention

- using silence
- referring to rights and responsibilities.

Reframing

The behaviour of a child with ADHD can be frustrating and annoying. But it's crucial for teachers to remember that he/she is not doing it on purpose; although there is no obvious physical disability, ADHD is a genuine medical condition.

Because these children and young people are so often in trouble, they are often unable to deal with criticism and can become defiant and hostile. This can damage their whole attitude to learning and to school and they may give up on education. We need to show that education has not given up on them and one technique to do this is called 'reframing'. This approach involves looking for the positives wherever possible, for example:

> Although you may be very frustrated at times, try to show patience and tolerance; there's every chance that the whole class will follow your example and the child with ADHD will be better supported and feel less isolated

- Regard the child who is easily distracted as 'having high levels of awareness and observation'
- Think of the restless child as being 'energetic and lively'
- When the child with ADHD goes off at a tangent, see it as 'a sign of individualism and independence'
- If the child forgets things, look at this as a result of him/her being 'absorbed in his/her own thoughts'
- If the child starts interrupting, regard it as 'enthusiasm to contribute'
- When work is sloppy, look for signs of effort despite difficulties, and remember that it may have cost this particular pupil a great deal of effort
- If homework hasn't been done or is handed in late, consider the possibility that the child was keen to do it well but frustrated by a lack of ability, support at home and/or time
- Look on a child's apparent selfishness as 'single-mindedness in pursuit of goals'.

Though some teachers will find this a difficult way of seeing the situation, this 'half-full' rather than 'half-empty' approach will help to maintain positive relationships with the child with ADHD. The most important behaviour in the class is that of the teacher and the way in which you respond to a child can strongly affect the way his/her classmates will behave towards him/her. Although you may be very frustrated at times, try to show patience and tolerance; there's every chance that the whole class will follow your example and the child with ADHD will be better supported and feel less isolated.

> In summary, behaviour management is what you want to make it. It can be frustrating but it can be fun: don't be gruff and fluffy, instead, be 'firm and fair'. Consistency and 'regretting the punishment' are the two essential keys to success.

Chapter 4

How can we help non-traditional learners to access the curriculum?

Children with ADHD will not always exhibit core symptoms in the classroom: much will depend on whether they are interested in the task, how the lesson is structured, and on the quality of support provided. However, as important as creative strategies are in enabling these 'non-traditional learners' to access the curriculum, the first step will always be the attitude of the teacher or supervisor with regards to working with students often perceived as difficult and disruptive.

The case studies below help to illustrate this point before I move on to some practical strategies for addressing the needs of children and young people with ADHD.

Case study 1: Jimmy McNally, Y4

The lesson objective was 'Making alternative clocks' for a group of Year 4 children who included Jimmy McNally. This involved the use of candles, water, sand, straws and a whole array of other materials.

Jimmy was one of the pupils who had to be carefully supervised and was known as a 'problem child'. He did not have any friends in the class and because of his general lack of empathy for others he was not popular amongst staff. He was often impulsive and hyperactive, and could be disruptive. Jimmy could also be verbally abusive to both peers and teachers.

On paper, the lesson plan for making alternative clocks appeared faultless and after a lengthy sermon to the students on the issue of health and safety, the stage was set. Not long after the lesson began the first problem observed was that of Tommy Craig's well-constructed Water Tower being inadvertently knocked over by Jimmy as he tried to create some extra room for his ever-expanding Sand Clock design. This led to a confrontation between an understandably aggrieved Tommy and Jimmy, as the latter tried to defend his actions that his construction 'needed more room'.

As the lesson moved on, my attention was drawn to Daisy Foster's science book which was now smouldering after Jimmy had also tried to move her Candle Clock down the table away from his project as his construction began to take on skyscraper proportions.

Meanwhile, Tom Jeffers' salt continued to pour furiously through the end of his 'Trump Tower' – now missing a bottom section (borrowed by Jimmy) in spite of Daisy, Tommy and a number of other pupils supplying extra layers of material in a highly collaborative team effort.

Though not as planned, we now had one specific construction that dominated the skyline but actually had a number of students working as a team in order to achieve a common objective . . . the Sand Clock also worked extremely well.

At the end of a tiring, yet successful lesson, Jimmy McNally rushed up to me as he left the room with his face streaked with grit, his hair soaking wet, shirt and tie hanging off him, and said: 'Thanks Sir this is the best lesson I've ever had'.

From that day forward, the teacher never had a major problem with Jimmy in class and whenever practical or project work was undertaken this previously unpopular individual had any number of pupils who wanted to be in his group.

Case study 2: Simon, Y9

Instead of being at Homework club after school, 13 year old Simon was spotted outside on the street on his skateboard. After being asked to come inside and join the others, Simon appeared flustered and disorientated and was finding it hard to settle at his desk. Also, his skateboard kept getting in his way. Though badly disorganised, Simon was usually a most passive and generally compliant student. After several minutes of watching him struggle to get started, the teacher suggested that he would remove Simon's skateboard until later. It came as a tremendous shock to the teacher when the boy's response was to jump out of his seat in a furious temper yelling,

'If you do that you'll be sorry!'

The room became a deadly hush apart from one child who whispered, 'Oh dear, Simon is in for it now.'

The key with Simon (who had ASD tendencies) was to be very specific about consequences, as in 'if you choose to do this, then this will be the outcome; if you choose to do that, then this will be the outcome'. Being very clear and specific about choices would be the key both with him and other students on the autistic spectrum.

Positive interventions

Once teachers and senior managers have an understanding of the specific needs of children and young people with ADHD, they can begin to try out specific strategies for ameliorating difficulties. In terms of day-to-day management of students with ADHD in the classroom, specific tried and trusted strategies are listed below (BOX 4a). In some cases this will simply confirm good practice,

---

BOX 4a Key strategies that should be employed with students who have ADHD

- Seat the student near to the teacher with his/her back to the rest of the class to keep other students out of view
- Surround the student with good role models, preferably those seen as 'significant others': facilitate peer tutoring, mentoring and cooperative learning
- Avoid distracting stimuli. Place the learner away from heaters/air conditioners, doors or windows, high traffic areas, computers
- Children with ADHD do not handle change well so minimise changes in schedule, physical relocation, disruptions; give plenty of warning when changes are about to occur
- Create a 'stimuli reduced area' for all students to access
- Maintain eye contact with the ADHD student during verbal instruction; avoid multiple commands/ requests
- Make directions clear and concise. Be consistent with daily instructions and expectations
- Give one task at a time and monitor frequently
- Make sure the student understands before beginning the task; repeat explanation in a calm, positive manner, if needed
- Help the child to feel comfortable with seeking assistance (most learners with ADHD won't ask)
- A child with ADHD may need more help for a longer period of time than the average child: gradually reduce assistance
- Use a day-book: make sure the student writes down assignments and both parents/teachers sign daily for homework tasks
- Modify assignments as necessary, developing an individualised programme; allow extra time when appropriate
- Make sure you are testing knowledge and understanding, not merely attention span.

but the key is to be consistent with the overall structure, while remaining flexible with some of the minor distractions and incidents that will occur.

Managing distractibility; dealing with fidgeting and improving concentration

One of the main areas teachers identify in working with children with ADHD is that they are easily distractible and that they will distract other children. Although teachers will differ in their views regarding the reasons for the distractibility, many of them will agree that children with ADHD become easily bored with classroom tasks and as a result look for other things to do, or other children to interact with. A key issue here is making sure that tasks are as interesting as possible and matched to the child's ability, presenting challenge but not so difficult that the child is defeated. Monitor progress and provide frequent encouragement as the work develops.

> The key is to be consistent with the overall structure, while remaining flexible with some of the minor distractions and incidents that will occur

Reduce the temptation for children to play with equipment on desks by insisting that all materials stay in bags placed on the floor or in lockers or personal pencil cases/trays. In younger classes, use pen tidies and book boxes in central desk arrangements.

Some children however, may benefit from having something to 'fiddle with'. One teacher that I met recently told me: '*I'm forever taking things off him; sometimes ten items a lesson . . . he taps his pencil, grinds his eraser into the desk . . . I take them away and a minute later he is playing with his watch strap*'. This story illustrates a crucial point which is that children with ADHD often need to manipulate something in those busy hands to help them to listen and focus, particularly in seated situations. You need to provide appropriate options for 'concentrators', such as allowing children to mould blu-tack or plasticine, or to use stress balls. I have even seen one teacher use a small pair of bar-magnets to help a child with major issues of overactivity in the classroom; this proved successful in reducing his fidgeting, so allowing him to concentrate more effectively. There is also a growing range of commercially produced items such as plastic spirals called *Tangles*. Whichever type of concentrator is favoured, some basic rules of use should be established at the outset. These might include items being issued at the start of the lesson and collected in at the end, with clear sanctions for misuse.

Research and practical experience has shown that children with ADHD need to have something to do to help them focus, especially in group listening activities. Appropriate 'concentrators' should almost certainly be used during sessions that have a lengthy listening component, such as the teacher reading to the whole class, class and whole school assemblies, Circle Time and the delivery of extensive instructions or directions (on field trips etc.).

Improving time spent on seat work and overall time management

One of the main issues to address with pupils who have ADHD, especially younger children, is how to improve the overall time spent on task. These children who appear overactive can find 'seat work' difficult to focus on and in addition, often appear to have no sense of time management regarding a learning activity.

Developing an appreciation of time is a particularly difficult skill for children with ADHD. One device that is very useful for improving concentration and developing a sense of time management is the humble egg timer. There are a number of ways that the timers can be used, such as:

- helping children to focus on a task by being aware of a time limit indicated by the sands trickling through

- enabling proactive movement by allowing the child to twist the timer after every cycle
- developing collaborative learning by sharing the timing of a task with a peer.

There is a good range of timers available, offering 1/3/5/10 minute cycles; these can be used selectively depending on the child's specific issues. In addition, they can be used as a time out tool for children who may need a break away from their table group or from the rest of the class.

> A key issue is making sure that tasks are as interesting as possible and matched to the child's ability – presenting challenge but not so difficult that the child is defeated

The advantage of egg timers is that they are noiseless and relatively inexpensive, but there are lots of alternative options including various types of stop clocks and electronic timers. The Attention Tracker (AT) is a small pyramid box that sits on a student's desk with a liquid crystal front and three lights. It provides a means of tracking a student's length of concentration by allowing points for each minute he or she is on task. This is monitored by the teacher who carries a remote control device (similar to the remote for a TV set) and can remove points if they see the child not on task.

Games

> Developing an appreciation of time is a particularly difficult skill for children with ADHD

Games such as 'statues' can help to focus children on being still and controlling their bodies. This is a game where the child sits 'like a statue' and tries to extend the time she/he can be motionless; the time can be displayed on a bar chart and rewarded by stickers or merits. Once learned, this activity can be practised alone by the child, and at home with the family and is therefore much more likely to provide a long-term solution to overactivity.

'Catch me if you can' is another game in which children can improve sitting and observation skills by counting for example, how many times a teacher may touch his nose during a set period of time.

'Beating the clock' is a way of helping children to develop an appreciation of time and the need to focus on a task within a set amount of time. Set a stopwatch to 5, 10 or 15 minute intervals and explain to the pupil that a specific task must be completed within the time allocated.

Endurance training

Ways of helping older students to develop periods of sustained controlled activity levels, which we could call 'endurance training', will involve gradually increasing the time and improving their ability to sit and complete tasks. This will often require the teacher to break down a lesson into short, clearly defined sessions. For example, a 40-minute lesson could be shaped as suggested in BOX 4b.

BOX 4b Dividing a 40-minute lesson into short, clearly defined sessions

1. To sit still during the 5–10 minute introduction to the lesson: the teacher then indicates part 1 is over
2. To focus on the individual/paired/group task: the teacher indicates part 2 is half-way through, then over
3. To get through the group discussion/plenary: the teacher indicates part 3 is over
4. To keep it together during the clear up time/giving of homework/preparation for next lesson: the teacher indicates part 4 is nearly over.

All of these activities or techniques to harness concentration and extend on-task behaviour will need to be practised with the child on a regular basis, with the teacher giving regular feedback to the child and parent on progress that is made. Targets may be included in a child's Individual Education Plan (IEP).

Developing basic skills

As children with ADHD may be very weak in a host of fundamental areas (40% of children with ADHD also have co-existing issues associated with Dyslexia (Germanò et al 2010)), some of the following suggestions may help in supporting their development of basic skills.

English skills and reading comprehension

- **Partner reading activities.** Pair the child with ADHD with another student partner who is a strong reader. The partners take turns reading orally, listening to each other and talking about the story or information.
- **Playacting.** Schedule playacting sessions where the child can role-play different characters from books read or stories shared: use short plays to read aloud (highlight specific parts to be read by the child).
- **Word bank.** Keep a word bank or dictionary of new or hard-to-read sight-vocabulary words.
- **Board games for reading comprehension.** Play board games that provide practice with target reading-comprehension skills or sight-vocabulary words.
- **Computer games for reading comprehension.** Schedule computer time for the child to have drill-and-practice with sight-vocabulary words.
- **Recorded books.** These materials, available from many libraries, can stimulate interest in reading and increase a child's confidence (consider asking the pupil to listen to the recorded reading then read out a selected section).
- **Back-up materials for home use.** Make available to students a second set of books and materials that they can use at home.
- **Summary materials.** Allow and encourage students to use published book summaries, synopses, and digests of major reading assignments to review (not replace) reading assignments.

Phonics

Most schools use a structured approach to teach phonics and the 'little and often' pattern can be effective with children who have ADHD. Lapses in concentration can result in a child missing a significant piece of learning in a fast-moving session however, so be vigilant in monitoring progress and ready to provide suitable revision where necessary.

Strategies such as '**Mnemonics for phonics**' can be useful. Teach the child mnemonics that provide reminders about hard-to-learn phonics rules (e.g., 'when two vowels go walking, the first does the talking'). Computer games can provide effective and enjoyable opportunities for 'drill and practice'.

> Set a stopwatch to 5, 10 or 15 minute intervals and explain to the pupil that a specific task must be completed within the time allocated

Writing

In composing stories or other writing assignments, children with ADHD benefit from the excellent practice found in English lessons in primary classrooms; some of this work may need to be revisited and revised at secondary level for students with ADHD who have not developed the relevant skills and understanding. Standard approaches may include:

- **clarifying, modelling, exemplifying** high standards for written work, with attention to format and style.
- **structuring a story** (e.g., plot, main characters, setting, conflict, and resolution) **and information text** (introduction, key points, sub headings etc.).
- **proofreading completed work.** Provide the student with a list of success criteria to check when proofreading his or her own work, or swap with a 'critical friend'.
- **alternative recording.** Ask the student to dictate writing assignments to a scribe, into a recorder, or use voice recognition software as an alternative to writing. Use a word processor sometimes, perhaps with software including predictive text to speed up the process.

Spelling

To help children with ADHD who are poor spellers, the following techniques have been found to be helpful:

- **Everyday examples of hard-to-spell words.** Take advantage of everyday events to teach spellings in context: for example, for a child who is quite confrontational in class, look at words like 'compromise', 'concede', 'acquiesce'.
- **'Look, Say, Cover, Write, Check':** use this approach consistently, throughout school.
- **Personal dictionary.** Ask the child to keep a personal dictionary of frequently misspelled words so that he/she can refer to the correct spelling quickly and easily.
- **Partner spelling activities.** Pair the child with another student. Ask the partners to quiz each other on the spelling of new words. Encourage both students to 'have a go' at the correct spelling. They can also play games such as 'hangman' and Scrabble.
- **Colour-coded letters.** Colour code different letters in hard-to-spell words (e.g., 'receipt') and draw attention to the 'tricky bits'.
- **Word banks.** Use index cards to store frequently misspelled words sorted alphabetically; or an alphabet sheet (A4, with boxes for words starting with each letter of the alphabet).

Maths computation

Numerous individualised instructional practices can help children with ADHD improve their basic computation skills. The following are just a few:

- **Partnering for maths activities.** Pair a child with ADHD with another student and provide opportunities for the partners to quiz each other about basic computation skills.
- **Language of maths.** If children do not understand the symbols and language used in maths, they will not be able to do the work. For instance, do they understand terms such as 'product' and 'quotient'? Provide a Maths dictionary or bank of key words.
- **Mnemonics for basic computation.** Teach the child mnemonics that describe basic steps in computing whole numbers. For example, 'Don't Miss Susie's Boat' can be used to help the student recall the basic steps in long division (i.e., divide, multiply, subtract, and bring down). SOCA for Sine-Opposite, Cosine-Adjacent.
- **Real-life examples.** Provide the child with real-life opportunities to practise measurement, time and money skills. For example, ask the child to calculate his or her change when paying for lunch in a cafeteria, or set up a class store where children can practise giving change. (Plastic money is fine for very young children but use real coins for older students if they are unable to deal in the abstract.)
- **Calculators to check basic computation.** Ask the child to use a calculator to check his or her working out, or to speed up lengthy problem-solving activities.

- **Board games for basic computation.** Ask the child to play board games to practise skills (such as 'Othello' or 'Connect 4').
- **Computer games for basic computation.** Schedule computer time for the child to practise basic computations, using appropriate software.

> Children with ADHD often need to manipulate something in those busy hands to help them to listen and focus, particularly in seated situations

Depending on the pupil's level of literacy and numeracy development, the support of a teaching assistant (TA) or learning support assistant (LSA) may be appropriate, or tuition from a specialist Dyslexia teacher. In these circumstances, it's important that the adult involved is familiar with the child's specific needs regarding ADHD, as well as the literacy/numeracy targets. Consistency between the classroom, and class teacher and other adults involved with the child is paramount.

Information and communication technology (ICT)

ICT is a constantly developing area where children with ADHD can find a non-threatening environment in which to achieve success. For many, learning may have become associated with the fear of failure, both in their own eyes and in the eyes of those around them. The computer (in any of its manifestations) can provide a neutral setting in which to experiment, with students confident that they are controlling the pace and level of work. As some learners with ADHD find it hard to establish relationships, and do not always easily relate to others, using a computer can avoid this problem, and can often offer an entry point for another person to join in alongside, in a non-threatening manner.

Having said this, it's important to acknowledge that multi-media options can also be problematic for risk-takers in terms of use of inappropriate sites, indulging in extensive and reckless online shopping etc. The issue of cyber bullying is also something that youngsters must be aware of and able to deal with. Careful monitoring and once again a degree of 'Structure' and 'Flexibility' are essential.

There is a vast array of ICT equipment to help students with ADHD. Devices such as hand-held spell checkers and calculators can support learners who have difficulties with sequencing and memorising. Multimedia technologies, which can present sounds, photographs and video, as well as text and graphics on the screen, provide new directions for working with all students who may have learning and behaviour difficulties. They are motivating, 'cool' and present opportunities for demonstrating what has been learned which are not so dependent on the (hand)written word.

Materials used will vary according to the techniques employed, but should always be as attractive and engaging as possible; and age-appropriate. There is no doubt that approaches involving ICT appear to relate well to the learning processes of children with ADHD for a number of reasons:

- the child responds well to an individualised or 1–1 setting
- attention is focused on the screen
- technology provides multi-sensory experiences
- computers are non-threatening and provide constant feedback and reinforcement
- a computer is impersonal – it doesn't yell, criticise or have favourites
- a variety of presentation styles ensures better attention
- students can control the pace and 'try again' if necessary
- computers are flexible in that they can be programmed to do many things, often at different levels and in different ways
- students can receive rapid, objective assessment

- game-like approaches appeal to pupils with ADHD and they enjoy the challenge.

Literacy and spelling programs such as the 'Active Literacy Kit' (and especially Units of Sound) appear particularly effective, along with Word Shark, Number Shark, Text Detective and a host of others in the market.

> There is no doubt that approaches involving ICT appear to relate well to the learning processes of children with ADHD

Study skills

Children with ADHD often have difficulty in learning how to study effectively on their own. The following strategies may assist them in developing the skills necessary for academic success:

- **Adapt worksheets.** Teach a child how to adapt instructional worksheets so that they don't seem overwhelming. For example, fold the worksheet to reveal only one question at a time, or use a piece of card or a ruler to cover some of the text and make it more manageable.
- **Diagrammatic recording.** Teach a child how to use Venn diagrams and mind maps to help illustrate and organise key concepts or pieces of information on a particular topic.
- **Note-taking skills.** Teach a child with ADHD how to take notes when organising key concepts that he or she has learned, perhaps with the use of a program such as 'Anita Archer's Skills for School Success'.
- **Checklist of frequent mistakes.** Provide the child with a checklist of mistakes that he or she frequently makes (e.g., punctuation or capitalisation errors in written assignments). Teach the child how to use this list when proofreading his or her work at home and school.
- **Uncluttered workspace.** Teach a child with ADHD how to prepare an uncluttered workspace to complete assignments. For example, instruct the child to clear away unnecessary books or other materials *before* beginning his or her seat work.
- **Monitor homework assignments.** Keep track of how well your students with ADHD cope with homework, discussing and resolving with them and their parents any problems in completing assignments.

> Children with ADHD often have difficulty in learning how to study effectively on their own

Homework

The considered opinion is that it takes a pupil with ADHD at least three times as long to do a piece of work at home as it would take to do in school. The many distractions of home and a more casual, unstructured environment mean that attention is less focused and therefore everything takes longer. It may be better for the child to do homework in a homework club if possible, but talking to parents or carers about homework and persuading them to be proactive in their support can make a big difference to the child. Encourage parents to:

- monitor homework set each day and take an interest; ask the child to explain what he or she has to do
- establish a routine time for the completion of homework (e.g. after tea, before the TV or games console is switched on; or first thing in the morning)
- minimise distractions (e.g. younger siblings)
- provide a clear surface in a quiet space.

> Keep track of how well your students with ADHD cope with homework, discussing and resolving with them and their parents any problems in completing assignments

With the time element in mind, teachers should differentiate homework to ensure that pupils with ADHD do not have to spend three times as long as peers on any given assignment. I know of one mother who, frustrated by the lack of help she received from her child's school with regards to his homework schedule, sent in the following note to one of his teachers:

Tuesday 7.15 am

'Dear Ms Brown

I am spending over 2 hours a night on Jason's homework . . . please find his laundry enclosed'.

Exam arrangements

For national examinations (e.g. SATs and GCSE), a whole host of special arrangements exist for students with a range of special needs, including ADHD. It is important that teachers know about all of the possibilities and how and when to apply for them. Practice in advance is also an essential requirement for success. Working with a reader (amanuensis) for example is a skilled technique and students will need to have at least three or four trials before attempting the exam if this strategy is to work well.

Current special arrangement options include:

- extra time allowance
- rest periods
- use of readers
- amanuensis
- word processors
- allowance for spelling, punctuation and grammar
- prompters.

In summary, there is no one-size-fits-all approach for supporting students with ADHD. Teachers will attempt their own strategies in delivering the curriculum, presenting the material and getting their students to complete tasks in a host of different ways.

The main target is that in every class the teacher specifies exact expectations, possibly in terms of:

- This is the work you **must** do
- This is the work you **should** do
- This is the work you **could** do.

'Must', has to mean **must** and no compromises, whether the child is ADHD or not. Failure to comply means that their right to attend the class might well be revised.

Educating the child with ADHD can be a difficult and demanding process but also an extremely fulfilling one. A child engaged and interested in the learning process is obviously much less likely to engage in other activities that will be regarded as poor or inappropriate behaviour.

Chapter 5

Whole school approaches

'Inclusion' has many definitions but essentially it is about every student having an entitlement to personal, social and intellectual development and being given an opportunity to achieve his/her potential. In keeping with this philosophy, educational systems should be designed to take into account the wide diversities that exist amongst the school population. Those pupils with exceptional learning needs and/or disabilities should have access to high quality and appropriate education. These worthy principles are difficult to achieve in practice however, with finite resources and a responsibility to provide for an ever-increasing range of complex difficulties within a mainstream classroom.

For children with ADHD this opens up a key debate, as these pupils will require a variety of options that may be beyond the budgets, and/or perhaps outside the culture, of the school (more about this in Chapter 7). Having said this, ADHD is clearly a condition that can be successfully managed in many schools and for this reason there is a tremendous cause for optimism. What makes a school successful in providing for children and young people with ADHD? I think this is best summed up as a multi-modal management model that I have observed in many schools.

A multi-modal model

Schools with a multi-modal approach employ the principles of 'SF3R'. In this acronym, S stands for 'Structure' which is in essence the values, rules and systems those children and young people need in order to make sense of the world around them. Structure allows children and young people to feel safe and creates security in their lives by developing clear boundaries and expectations.

> SF3R = Structure, Flexibility, Rapport, Relationships and Role models

F stands for 'Flexibility', where adaptation to a range of different circumstances will complement the structure in children's lives and allow freedom, opportunity and fun for all involved. Effective flexibility requires an appreciation of different people and cultures and an understanding that fairness is not giving everyone the same, but giving people what they need.

The 3Rs stand for 'Rapport, Relationships and Role models' which are the means of selling, supporting and sustaining the long-term success of a structured yet flexible approach.

Structure

This encompasses many aspects of the organisational structures of the school and includes four key areas:

- leadership and management
- teaching and learning targets
- behaviour expectations and application of rules
- general classroom management.

> Structure allows children and young people to feel safe and creates security in their lives by developing clear boundaries and expectations

Leadership and management

It needs to be clearly stated that overall success in the management of ADHD will only be achieved through effective leadership and management. SENCOs play a key role in this. They should be included in the Senior Management Team (SMT) and be in a position to influence strategy, as well as having the status to develop good practice with regard to managing pupils with ADHD (and other special educational needs) among the teaching, non-teaching and care/support staff in the school. The delivery of a focused and consistent approach throughout is essential if pupils with ADHD are to thrive; this requires ongoing monitoring, evaluation and development, and the SENCO will usually be the professional best placed to fulfil this function. Part of this process involves the selection and retention of proactive support staff, geared towards supporting the needs of children with ADHD. Choosing appropriate individuals, with the patience and personality to deal with children with ADHD is critical and hanging on to them once found, is vital. It's important to provide ongoing support for them as they deal with the daily and often emotionally draining challenge of ADHD, as well as encouraging and facilitating their continuing professional development.

Teaching and learning targets, behaviour expectations and general classroom management strategies have already been covered in previous chapters; however, the key issue is that the environment should be adapted (where possible) to the needs of the child, rather than the child being expected to adapt to an inflexible environment.

Flexibility

A solid overall structure needs to be complemented by flexibility in the management of learning and behaviour in order to achieve success with children with ADHD.

The following areas will need to be addressed as whole school issues:

> The delivery of a focused and consistent approach throughout is essential if pupils with ADHD are to thrive

- differentiation of the curriculum
- support for skills development
- management of rewards and sanctions
- systems for non-structured time
- working with outside agencies.

The first three areas have been covered in earlier chapters and so let us look at the last two.

Non-structured time

Non-structured or out-of-classroom time such as breaks and lunchtimes, is an area for careful consideration by senior management. It is a myth that 'letting loose' a child with ADHD will allow him or her to run off all of his excess energy at break time. In practice, the child is often unable to control his or her impulsive and hyperactive symptoms and chaos occurs, leading to a number of 'incident reports' and trips to the head teacher before afternoon registration. SENCOs should have a 'Plan B' for these times with the option of structured activities available indoors for selected pupils. This might include interest clubs, computer group, eco-activities (such as litter-picking and recycling) or a 'monitor' role that involves preparation of resources and equipment for afternoon lessons. Peer- tutoring or helping out with younger children can also work well.

'Friendship stops' are established in many primary schools, where a child can wait to be befriended when feeling lonely, sad or just left-out. The success of these depends on a strong supportive ethos amongst pupils, and perhaps some responsible children designated as 'buddies'. These youngsters are alert to anyone standing at a 'stop' and needing support during playtimes; they may also be tasked (on a rota basis) with partnering a child with ADHD on a specific day.

A buddy system works best when participating children receive some training, with clear guidelines and expectations, and some recognition of/reward for, their endeavours.

Playground supervisors are often tasked nowadays with teaching children how to play organised games, thus helping to develop good social skills such as turn-taking and working in a team, as well as ensuring good exercise. Training with regards to ADHD management will enhance supervisors' skills and enable them to be as effective as possible with children who find it difficult to 'stand still and listen'.

> Part of an effective approach is the selection and retention of proactive support staff, geared towards supporting the needs of children with ADHD

Working with outside agencies

Coping with an array of behavioural, emotional and social needs can present a huge challenge to school staff who may feel that this falls outside their area of knowledge and expertise. In this situation, outside agencies may be called upon to support the teaching and management of children with ADHD. These may be:

- local authority services delivering CPD sessions to staff
- behavioural support professionals offering 'hands on' support in the classroom, modelling effective strategies which the teacher and TA can observe and evaluate
- an educational psychologist
- a trained mentor/counselor.

Training courses offered outside school by specialist organisations such as ADDISS (www.addiss.co.uk) may also be of valuable assistance.

Where a child's difficulties are causing, or adding to problems at home, it may be helpful to involve professionals from health and/or social services in working directly with parents (more about this in Chapter 8).

Another aspect of 'flexibility' is the option of medication as part of the treatment plan. This should be considered

> Where a child's difficulties are causing, or adding to problems at home, it may be helpful to involve professionals from health and/or social services in working directly with parents

jointly by health agencies, SENCO and family, with all parties keeping an open mind about the feasibility of medication being used to support the child. (The issue of medication in terms of management of ADHD will be considered in the next chapter.)

Rapport, Relationships, Role models

The 3Rs support and sustain Structure and Flexibility.

Rapport

Setting up a range of proactive systems, structures and strategies to teach and manage children with ADHD is all very well but what if the children won't let you work with them because they are resistant to change? The solution lies in developing an effective rapport with distracted, disruptive and disillusioned children. This means establishing a relationship of two or more people who are *'in sync'* or on the *'same wavelength'*: they understand and can relate well to each other. (The word 'rapport' stems from an old French verb 'rapporter' which means literally to carry something back i.e. share similar values, beliefs, knowledge and interests.)

Developing rapport with children who have ADHD may not always be straightforward, however, and some of these individuals will make it hard work. Some points to consider include:

- teachers assessing their own feelings when working with challenging children and being able to 'detach' the behaviour from the child

- understanding that the way in which teachers behave towards a child often influences the way that other children react towards him or her.

> The solution lies in developing an effective rapport with distracted, disruptive and disillusioned children

The key is to find something that you and the child can share; this might be an interest in football, computer games or cooking, a dislike of something, or a shared difficulty – with spelling, for example. A personal connection is vital in developing rapport and mutual trust.

Relationships

Every one of us has feelings, but not all of us find it easy to share those feelings with others. Being able to communicate in this way, with both classmates and teachers, is an important part of any child's development, but a particularly valuable asset in coping with ADHD. Helping a child to recognise, name and describe his/her emotions is key to helping him or her to understand and manage his/her condition.

Many schools incorporate 'emotional literacy' in their PSHE curriculum and much can be achieved in circle time and tutor groups to develop empathy and interpersonal skills, as well as improving self-esteem and intra-personal understanding. For some children with ADHD, appropriate mentoring can provide this type of support; with training, a HLTA (Higher Level Teaching Assistant) or an older pupil in the school may be able to fulfil this function very successfully. In cases where more deep-seated emotional and socialisation issues exist however, specialist counselling may be required.

It is outside the scope of this book to fully describe the kind of counselling specialism necessary to support often very complex situations, but it is a vital option to consider (see Chapter 7 for more about counselling). It is also important to add that within the philosophy of 'it takes a village to raise a child', it is often the case that a child needs to hear the same or similar messages or advice from a different source in addition to the front line teacher or SENCO in order to take it on board: sometimes, an 'unfamiliar' source of advice has more resonance than someone close to us. In a similar way, parents may be exasperated when their child appears not to have heard or accepted their advice on a certain matter, only to nod in agreement when their grandparent delivers a similar piece of wisdom. This effect is of course, amplified a hundred-fold when the 'wisdom' comes from the mouth of a respected peer, sporting champion or any sort of 'hero' with celebrity status! (See 'role models' below.)

Even when an intervention such as mentoring or counselling is being provided, the everyday interaction of teachers and TAs with children who have ADHD, is an important element of a school's provision. It can be valuable to remind colleagues of the effectiveness of a positive approach at all times in building and sustaining sound relationships with pupils and the responses suggested in the box below (BOX 5a), provide ideas for appropriately-worded comments.

> Helping a child to recognise, name and describe his emotions is key to helping him understand and manage his condition

Peer to peer interaction

One of the key areas to consider will be how to develop relationships between children with ADHD and other pupils. Children with ADHD can often find it difficult to make and

BOX 5a Using positive comments to build and sustain good pupil–teacher relationships

Following rules and routines

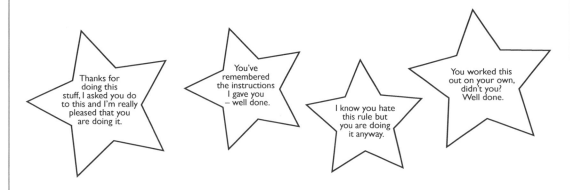

Thanks for doing this stuff, I asked you do to this and I'm really pleased that you are doing it.

You've remembered the instructions I gave you – well done.

I know you hate this rule but you are doing it anyway.

You worked this out on your own, didn't you? Well done.

Giving feedback

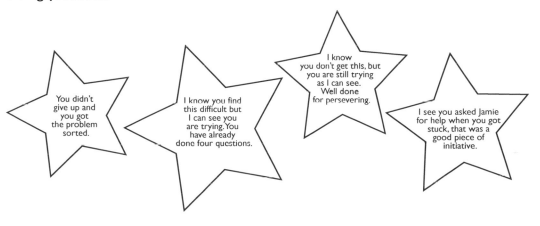

You didn't give up and you got the problem sorted.

I know you find this difficult but I can see you are trying. You have already done four questions.

I know you don't get this, but you are still trying as I can see. Well done for persevering.

I see you asked Jamie for help when you got stuck, that was a good piece of initiative.

Accepting other people's views

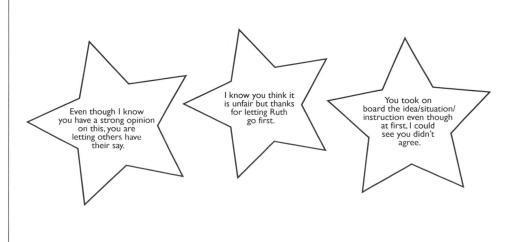

Even though I know you have a strong opinion on this, you are letting others have their say.

I know you think it is unfair but thanks for letting Ruth go first.

You took on board the idea/situation/instruction even though at first, I could see you didn't agree.

keep friends as their hyperactive and impulsive symptoms often prevent long-lasting relationships from being formed. Sadly, children with ADHD will seldom be invited to birthday parties, play-dates or sleepovers at other houses as they are often marked out as 'problem children' among parents. This can result in a worsening of the situation since they then have few opportunities to experience social situations, observe good role models and develop their own skills.

These factors may lead in some cases to children with ADHD being bullied, though they may be 'provocative victims': this obviously exacerbates problems of socialization and can lead to difficulties between families as well as between individual children. Educating children about different special needs and explaining the difficulties that some people experience can go a long way to improving their tolerance and understanding. A colleague told me about her four-year-old grand-daughter who often came out of school talking about 'Jason' and describing some of the 'naughty' things he had done that day. After a few weeks in Reception however, Abby was developing a different perspective on things: '*Do you know Nana, Jason can't help it. He's not really naughty, he just can't help it.*' A wise early-years practitioner had nipped this particular stigmatisation 'in the bud'; after a while, Jason was never mentioned and when asked, Abby would report only that he was '*OK*'.

> It is often the case that a child needs to hear the same or similar messages or advice from a different source in addition to the front line teacher or SENCO

School staff and SENCOs cannot be expected to create friendships amongst children but they do have a responsibility to promote inclusion of non-traditional learners, such as children with ADHD. Depending on the age and stage of the children, relationships within the class can be developed by means of approaches such as:

- Circle Time
- PSHE/Citizenship lessons
- drama and role play
- social stories
- peer mediation.

As in all areas, patience and an understanding of needs will be required to drive success in developing peer to peer relationships.

Role models

All staff should see themselves as positive role models for pupils, but this is particularly important for a minority of children with ADHD who have decided that school is not for them; they do not trust adults and set out to be 'the best that they can be at being the worst that they can be'.

These individuals are much more likely to be involved in both fixed-term and permanent exclusions affording them more 'unstructured time' in which they may become prey to various negative influences. Some of these natural 'risk-takers' will be attracted to antisocial activities. The Youth Justice Board (2008) states that ADHD is one of the highest risk factors for youth offending: individuals with ADHD with their non-premeditated, impulsive and hyperactive characteristics become the 'followers' rather than the 'leaders' of street gangs and are much more likely to be caught than their more calculating more premeditated colleagues.

> Directing children with ADHD into more productive activities should not only be encouraged, but proactively directed in some cases in order to prevent negative outcomes

Directing children with ADHD into more productive activities should not only be encouraged, but proactively directed in some cases in order to prevent negative outcomes.

Some of the more positive 'gangs' could well be sports-orientated (not just football but martial arts, gymnastics, dance etc.), music or drama, whereby positive role models can influence young people. Inviting past pupils into school to talk about their successful careers and experiences can also inspire and motivate pupils and give them a clearer image of what, how, who they want to be.

A useful activity with pupils who have ADHD can be to research famous people known to have or to have had the disorder. It is claimed that rock star Kurt Cobain, Lord Byron, Oscar Wilde, Picasso and Sir Walter Raleigh all shared such a developmental disorder.

Others include Jules Verne, Mark Twain, guerilla leader Che Guevara, and actors James Dean and Clark Gable. Such research can reassure pupils that they are not alone in their experiences and difficulties, and that, importantly, ADHD need not stand in the way of high achievement.

> A student with ADHD was asked what it takes to be a good role model and said . . . *'Someone who does the right things at the right time for the right reasons'*

Within schools of course, teachers and SENCOs will always try to create positive influences but knowing what makes a 'good' role model is difficult to answer. One student with ADHD when asked which teacher he most admired, said the reason for naming one particular individual was that *'you know where you are with him'*.

As general guidelines, members of staff could consider the following dimensions in presenting an effective teaching role model:

- the way that you present yourself and the reputation you acquire
- the tone and boundaries that you set
- the level and consistency of your discipline, and demonstration of 'fairness'
- the way in which you personalise your teaching and hone your skills in the production of interesting and motivating lessons
- your interaction with other staff, and how you model patience, appreciation and good manners.

A student with ADHD was asked what it takes to be a good role model and he said the following . . . *'Someone who does the right things at the right time for the right reasons'*.

You can't put it better than that!

In summary, students with ADHD can be included very successfully in mainstream education when schools have appropriate systems and a supportive ethos. All staff should receive training on ADHD and understand how structure, flexibility and good relationships can combine to maximize the learning opportunities of pupils with this condition.

Chapter 6

How does medication help?

The use of medication for helping children with ADHD has suffered from significantly 'bad press' in recent years. Inappropriate prescription and adverse side effects always make for shocking 'scare stories'. But in fact, carefully prescribed and administered medication can transform the lives of some youngsters and those of their families, allowing them to lead more enjoyable and satisfying lives.

> Carefully prescribed and administered medication can transform the lives of some youngsters and those of their families

Medication will always remain a controversial issue and it is never an easy decision for any family to take. However, when it works medication can have very positive effects, as described in the case study below.

Case study: a mother describes the positive effects of medication for her child with ADHD

I had never heard of ADHD, and, in fact, it is common for the condition to go undiagnosed in many of its sufferers. But the difficulty of diagnosis is not matched by a difficulty in treatment. The effects of appropriate medication combined with counselling and support can be so profound as to seem almost magical.

A special needs child can influence the harmony of the entire family. When you have a child with an undiagnosed disorder you can be sure you will have conflict between husband and wife and constant struggle between siblings. Different rules apply to special needs children. For the first time in years, now that my daughter is on the right track and I have a sense of what I am dealing with we argue less and get along much better. I am much less exasperated because I can see things from her perspective and I know I am a good mother and that she is not purposely trying to drive me bananas. I can often ask her to do something without getting much argument in return – something I could never do before.

(Herman 1999)

Different types of medication

Essentially there are two main kinds of treatment for ADHD which we can classify as:

Stimulants: Methylphenidate and Dexamphetamine

Non Stimulants: Atomoxetine

Other medication options which are sometimes considered in the treatment and management of ADHD include Clonidine, Risperidone, Melatonin and some types of antidepressants.

Methylphenidate is thought to increase the levels of a chemical messenger, dopamine, in the brain; this appears to reduce hyperactivity and impulsivity and promote attentiveness. Methylphenidate exists in both short-acting forms lasting 3–4 hours and long-acting forms (Concerta XL, Equasym XL and Medikinet XL) which last for extended periods during the day. The effects of these are highlighted in the table below along with some other medication options. Possible side effects of Methylphenidate can include loss of appetite (common but transient); inability to sleep; nervousness. Headaches and stomach pains can also occur.

> Monitoring both the effect of the medication in addressing behaviour and any potential side effects will need full co-operation between teachers, health professionals and parents

Atomoxetine works differently from Methylphenidate. It increases the level of the chemical messenger Noradrenalin (a natural chemical in the brain) thereby addressing ADHD symptoms for those for whom it is effective. Response to Atomoxetine is usually within two weeks but maximum effect may not occur till after 6 to 8 weeks. Benefits include a positive effect on mood and sleep, with a reduction in anxiety. Side effects can result in a lack of appetite and tummy ache, though this is often mild.

Monitoring both the effect of the medication in addressing behaviour and any potential side effects will need full cooperation between teachers, health professionals and parents. Schools should have their own medicines policy for the storage and administration of all medicines including those for treating ADHD. There is useful general guidance entitled 'Managing Medicines in School and Early Years settings (March 2005)' available from the DfE.

Medication chart for ADHD treatment (Note XL means Extended Release)			
Drug	**Trade name**	**Length of effect**	**Principal effect**
Methylphenidate	Ritalin	4 hrs	Improves concentration and lessens hyperactivity
	Medikinet	4 hrs	Improves concentration and lessens hyperactivity
	Medikinet XL	8 hrs	Improves concentration and lessens hyperactivity
	Equasym XL	8 hrs	Improves concentration and lessens hyperactivity
	Concerta XL	10–12 hrs	Improves concentration and lessens hyperactivity
Dexamphetamine	Dexedrine	4 hrs	Improves concentration
Lisdexamfetamine dimesylate	Elvanse	13 hrs	Improves concentration and lessens hyperactivity
Clonidine	Dixarit	4–6 hrs	Improves impulsivity and lessens angry outbursts
Risperidone	Risperdal	12 hrs	Lessens angry outbursts
Melatonin		2 hrs	Helps to settle to sleep
Atomoxetine	Strattera	3 hrs in blood stream, 24 hour effect in the brain	Improves concentration and lessens impulsivity

Each individual child with ADHD will respond differently to medication, however certain patterns have developed between the two main groups in use today in the UK, i.e. the stimulants and the non stimulant Atomoxetine. A list of potential advantages and disadvantages of each are shown below (BOX 6a).

BOX 6a Advantages and disadvantages of stimulants and non stimulants in the treatment of ADHD

Advantages

Disadvantages

Stimulants

- Rapid onset of action, benefits may be noted in the first few days
- Short duration of action; can be used for just school hours and not weekends
- Long acting (8 hour and 12 hour) tablets available
- Easy to adjust dose to fit circumstances
- Long track record with good safety profile

- Controlled drug; requires hand written prescriptions or typed with specific details
- Potential for abuse by others (much less likely with long acting XL formulations)
- Can suddenly wear off at inconvenient times (short acting tablets need to be repeated at lunchtime in school)
- Can have side effects including significant appetite suppression or poor sleep
- Work only when given; i.e. each morning the child acts as though medication has never been given

Atomoxetine

- Not a controlled drug and absolutely no abuse potential
- Once (or twice) daily dosing with 24 hour duration of action
- Much less appetite suppression and better sleeping at night
- Benefit continues into next day even if a dose is late or forgotten
- Licensed for children and adolescents (and adults taking the medication as adolescents)

- This is a new drug without a long track record
- Can cause abdominal complaints in 20% of children (eased by taking with food)
- Slow onset of action; can take 4 weeks to see benefit and 12 weeks to reach maximum
- The medication cannot be 'turned-off' for short periods, i.e. weekends and holidays
- Very rarely, it can cause aggression and disruptive behaviour

---

Teachers and support professionals should be aware that although medication is sometimes a very effective option, it is only one of the tools available in the management of ADHD. It does not 'cure' children with ADHD but may alleviate symptoms and enable them to concentrate and learn more effectively.

An argument for using medication

Although many teachers are very sceptical about the use of medication, an explanation of ADHD in medical terms can help them accept this as an option. ADHD can be described as a neurobiochemical condition caused by dysfunction of specific neurotransmitters within the brain. It is an accepted fact that these neurotransmitters are responsible for relaying information between and among various parts of the brain necessary for certain functions to take place (e.g. impulse control and concentration). Dysregulation in this complex chemical relay system can cause emotional and behavioural problems. As stated by Cooper in 1995 *medication is employed not as a chemical cosh to sedate overactive or inattentive children but as a chemical facilitator that raises chronically low levels of activity in certain parts of the brain and so regulates the message carrying process*.

> Teachers and support professionals should be aware that although medication is sometimes a very effective option, it is only one of the tools available in the management of ADHD

Few children with ADHD will actually enjoy taking medication, even though it may be helping them academically, behaviourally and socially. Some students do not like to feel different and they can also be embarrassed by other people (especially peers) knowing that they take medicine. In addition, a minority of students may suffer from minor side effects such as stomach upsets, especially in the early stages of treatment.

The best way of handling these issues is for the child to meet with the supervising specialist, either paediatrician or psychiatrist, to review the situation and discuss the options. Ideally, the child or adolescent should be positive about trying this course of action. In addition, the decision about whether or not to prescribe medication will also depend on a judgment of benefits versus the costs. Once a course of treatment is in progress, any side effects can usually be eradicated by minor changes in dosage or by changing the time the pills are administered.

For any child on medication, the communication between the family, physician and the school will be crucial. Although the decision as to whether or not medication is prescribed is with the physician, the role of the family working with the SENCO is essential to monitoring successful outcomes and reassuring the child about confidentiality within the school context.

> Medication does not 'cure' children with ADHD but may alleviate symptoms and enable them to concentrate and learn more effectively

Considering the medication process

Parents may well discuss the option of medication for their child with an empathetic teacher or SENCO before considering approaching their GP. Review meetings for IEPs are often occasions when the subject comes up. How then, can school staff inform parents and help them in considering the options? The guidelines below may prove useful in preliminary discussions.

When should medication be used?

Only after comprehensive evaluation and in circumstances where:

- earnest attempts at non-medical interventions have proved insufficient
- the child is at risk of emotional and/or academic failure
- a child is at significant risk of harming himself or others.

What is the process towards medication use for ADHD?

1. Observations made by teachers and parents; information passed to educational psychologist/clinician
2. Assessment and diagnosis
3. A structured learning environment is provided
4. Monitoring is carried out
5. The decision is made to seek medication

> Once a course of treatment is in progress, any side effects can usually be eradicated by minor changes in dosage or by changing the time the pills are administered

6. A base rate is established (to understand exactly which dosage and which specific medication is suitable for the child)
7. Trial of medication
8. Any side effects reported and necessary adjustments are made
9. Benefits presented
10. The situation is evaluated: regular reviews will be necessary to establish how maturation may affect the dose required and to measure all other indicators of normal health, as well as any side effects of the medication.

How can medications help people with ADHD?

They can:

- enhance attention
- improve self-control
- reduce extraneous activity
- improve academic performance
- improve handwriting
- improve motivation.

BOX 6b Responses to stimulant medications

Children with ADHD: 70–80% positive
Adults with ADHD: 60–70% positive
Less positive if there are co-existing conditions
Less positive for 'inattentive' type

Is medication alone an effective way forward?

While not all children having ADHD are prescribed medication, in certain cases it can play an important and necessary part in the child's overall treatment. However, the use of medication alone in treating ADHD is not recommended. As indicated earlier, a multi-modal plan is usually the best way forward. Recently updated NICE guidance (National Institute of Clinical Excellence) includes the following advice:

- Healthcare professionals should offer parents or carers of pre-school children with ADHD a referral to a parent-training/education programme as the first-line treatment if the parents or carers have not already attended such a programme or the programme has had a limited effect.
- Teachers who have received training about ADHD and its management should provide behavioural interventions in the classroom to help children and young people with ADHD.
- If the child or young person with ADHD has moderate levels of impairment, the parents or carers should be offered referral to a group parent-training/education programme, either on its own or together with a group treatment programme (cognitive behavioural therapy [CBT] and/or social skills training) for the child or young person.

However, the guidance supports the early use of medication for children with significant problems:

'In school-age children and young people with severe ADHD, drug treatment should be offered as the first-line treatment'

as part of a multi-modal approach:

'Drug treatment for children and young people with ADHD should always form part of a comprehensive treatment plan that includes psychological, behavioural and educational advice and interventions.'

(National Institute of Clinical Excellence 2009)

> '. . . medication can and should be used to improve the outcomes of individuals who suffer with ADHD symptoms.' (NICE 2009)

What is the SENCO's and teacher's role in the medication trial?

Teachers should be fully aware of the medical trial, looking out for and reporting side effects and reporting changes over time. Any signs of tics, withdrawal, odd behaviour or poor health should be reported immediately even if the teacher is unsure about the problem or is worried about being wrong.

Also teachers should be aware that for example although a child could be on a long-acting Methylphenidate, different formulations might be more effective at different ages and stages of the child.

The majority of children and young people with ADHD manage to avoid having to take medication during the school day, but there are exceptions to this. In many schools, specific staff, often TAs, are designated to manage the storage and administration of medicines as part of their role. Specific training is essential for this, with careful records kept and

> Although the decision as to whether or not medication is prescribed is with the physician, the role of the family working with the SENCO is essential to monitoring successful outcomes and reassuring the child about confidentiality within the school context

Chart showing the extended release formulations and the breakdown of the medication by type of Methylphenidate and different concentrations											
Medication	Medikinet XL (capsule) IR: ER 50:50					Equasym XL (capsule) IR:ER 30:70			Concerta XL (tablet) IR:ER 22:78		
Tablet/ capsule strength	5 mg	10 mg	20 mg	30 mg	40 mg	10 mg	20 mg	30 mg	18 mg	27 mg	36 mg
IR Proportion (Immediate Release) MPH	2.5 mg	5 mg	10 mg	15 mg	20 mg	3 mg	6 mg	9 mg	4 mg	6 mg	8 mg
ER Proportion (Extended Release) MPH	2.5 mg	5 mg	10 mg	15 mg	20 mg	7 mg	14 mg	21 mg	14 mg	21 mg	28 mg

strict safety precautions. Certainly for the purpose of planning residential trips including these children, additional forethought will be needed.

Over and above the school's general health and safety policy, there needs to be a policy for managing any medicines that children need to take while in school and while in the care of teaching staff out of school. 'Managing medicines in schools and early years settings' (DfES/Department of Health, 2005 (http://www.teachfind.com/national-strategies/guidance-managing-medicines-schools-and-early-years-settings)) explains various roles and responsibilities and advises on confidentiality, record keeping and the storage, access and disposal of medicines. (See Appendix 3 for permission and policy guidelines.)

What do parents need to know about medication?

Tired and anxious parents and carers may struggle with the idea of seeking medication for their child. Is it an acceptance of failure on their part? Will they be condemning their child to unpleasant side effects and a zombie-like existence? There is much that SENCOs and teachers can say to reassure parents and support them in their decision to approach the GP and explore the options for medication. Some basic facts to be shared are listed below.

- Medication, while it needs to be handled wisely, can be administered safely and effectively
- Medication does not make children into 'zombies' or dwarfs
- Stimulants are non-addictive and do not produce a 'high'
- Medication should always be considered in a child with significant ADHD
- There is currently significant under-medication in the UK
- Take time to look into the rationale for using medication and the facts about side effects
- Fine-tuning of dosage both in quality and timing is essential for effective management
- Combinations of medications are sometimes necessary in complex cases.

Children's perceptions

'Drug treatment for children and young people with ADHD should always form part of a comprehensive treatment plan that includes psychological, behavioural and educational advice and interventions'

Finally and most importantly, we have to consider what children themselves feel about medication. The VOICES study (Voices On Identity, Childhood, Ethics & Stimulants: Children join the debate, 2011) investigated children's experiences with ADHD diagnosis and stimulant drug treatments. Over 150 children in the United States and the United Kingdom were surveyed, recruited from NHS Trusts, university clinics and community paediatric centres.

Their attitudes, thoughts, hopes and fears have been beautifully captured in a cartoon trailer with the actual voices of children with ADHD entitled 'ADHD and me' and the whole study is well worth a look: http://www.adhdvoices.com/adhdvideos/adhdandme.shtml (accessed June 2013).

In summary, the option of medication is an extremely useful tool in the teaching and management of children and adolescents with ADHD. Both teachers and parents should discover and carefully consider the facts about different types of medication, rather than be misled by what they may read in the popular press. It's important to remember that the effective treatment of ADHD may need a combination of different approaches.

Chapter 7

Are there any additional options for managing ADHD?

Alongside the key approaches of educational intervention, behaviour management and medication, a host of supporting options exist in the management of children with ADHD. In this chapter we will consider a range of those options, all of which can be effective in addressing specific issues.

Cognitive-behavioural therapy (CBT)

Cognitive-behavioural therapy was developed 40 years ago and has proven to be effective in treating anxiety, behaviour problems and depression. Most medical professionals do not believe that CBT should replace an effective medication regime for ADHD but research suggests that it works better for ADHD than do other forms of therapy. One recent study, from Boston's Massachusetts General Hospital, found that a combination of medication and CBT was more effective at controlling ADHD symptoms than medication alone.

'*CBT picks up where medication leaves off*', says Steven A. Safren, Ph.D., leader of the study and assistant professor of psychology at Harvard University. '*Even after optimal treatment with medication, most individuals have residual symptoms, and this treatment appears to make them better.*'

Results can be achieved quite quickly. Traditional forms of therapy can go on for years, whereas cognitive-behavioural therapy typically yields its benefits in only 12 to 15 one-hour sessions. The focus is on thinking about the way in which transient thoughts and enduring beliefs about oneself affect how one feels and acts. It's a tool for getting organised, staying focused and improving one's ability to try to manage emotions and get along with others.

> Cognitive-behavioural therapy typically yields its benefits in only 12 to 15 one-hour sessions. It's a tool for getting organised, staying focused and improving one's ability to try to manage emotions and get along with others

CBT attempts to re-structure distorted patterns of thinking such as:

- **All-or-nothing thinking.** You view everything as entirely good or entirely bad: if you don't do something perfectly, you've failed.
- **Overgeneralisation.** You see a single negative event as part of a pattern: for example, you **always** forget your maths homework.
- **Mind reading.** You think you know what people think about you or about something you've done, and it's bad.
- **Fortune telling.** You are certain that things will turn out badly.
- **Magnification and minimisation.** You exaggerate the significance of minor problems while trivialising your accomplishments.
- **'Should' statements.** You focus on how things **should** be, leading to severe self-criticism as well as feelings of resentment toward others.
- **Personalisation.** You blame yourself for negative events and downplay the responsibility of others.

- **Mental filtering.** You see only the negative aspects of any experience.
- **Emotional reasoning.** You assume that your negative feelings reflect reality: feeling bad about your school work means 'I'm doing badly and will probably fail my exams'.
- **Comparative thinking.** You measure yourself against others and feel inferior, even though the comparison may be unrealistic.

CBT teaches ways of recognising distorted thoughts in order to replace them with realistic thinking.

'*Understanding how you think is an effective start to making changes in your life*', says J. Russell Ramsay, Ph.D., assistant professor of psychology at the University of Pennsylvania. '*Changing thoughts and changing behaviour work hand in hand and widening your view of a situation makes it possible to expand the ways you can deal with it*' (Low 2011).

Counselling

It would appear that changes in society may have reduced the opportunities available to young people to have someone with whom to discuss, formalise and clarify their thinking, especially those students with learning and behavioural difficulties. Parents are often fully occupied with work and the practicalities of running a household, and members of the extended family such as grandparents often live far away. Providing these opportunities within school has been achieved informally through initiatives such as Circle Time and PSHE discussion, but with the child who needs more personal and individual support this assistance can be patchy. Increasing pressure in schools has meant that often, teachers do not have the time to implement individual responses and, many would argue, lack the specific training and skills to undertake this task.

Counselling is a process which assists the individual concerned to focus upon his or her concerns while simultaneously exploring problems, making choices, managing crises and working through feelings of conflict. It allows children and young people to gain a better understanding of themselves and situations as well as developing strategies to manage change.

In schools, counselling can provide a cost-effective service for pupils experiencing emotional distress and/or behavioural problems, as a result of stress arising from relationship difficulties, loss and anxiety. When emotional distress is not addressed, tension can build up leading to deterioration in a pupil's attitude and mental stamina. These difficulties can contribute to truancy, reduced school performance and disaffection.

> Counselling is a process which assists the individual concerned to focus upon their concerns while simultaneously exploring problems, making choices, managing crises and working through feelings of conflict

Emotional well-being is clearly correlated with ADHD and it is not possible for schools to improve learning outcomes and the inclusion of all pupils, without considering the impact of emotional stress on attainment.

The DfE describes counselling as an important element of support for children and young people with emotional and behavioural difficulties (Department for Education, 2011). In its guidance aimed at promoting positive mental health, counselling is recognised as an important early intervention and preventive strategy to reduce pupils' stress levels. In parallel, OFSTED has consistently referred to counselling in schools as 'complementing pastoral care systems, supporting the management of pupils with emotional and behavioural difficulties and supporting effective child protection procedures'.

Counselling is likely to benefit a pupil with ADHD who

- demonstrates extreme mood swings
- shows indicators of school refusal
- bullies or is bullied

- may have experienced abuse
- indicates emotional responses to stress, e.g. self-harming, eating disorders etc.

The purpose of counselling is to support pupils sufficiently to allow them to function effectively, access the curriculum and engage with the activities offered within school. It is important to make the distinction, however, between the informal counselling skills used by staff in schools, and the process of counselling used by trained and qualified counsellors. As issues that may arise could be highly sensitive, it is important to use trained and accountable practitioners as counsellors in schools.

However effective it might be in theory, it would be difficult in practice to combine the role of counsellor with that of teacher as the two roles may conflict in terms of different expectations of discipline for example, and in the manner of liaising with parents. The necessity to establish equality of status between counsellor and client can also lead to problems when the two roles are combined. For a combination of these reasons, most schools employ or 'buy-in' qualified counsellors.

> In DfE guidance aimed at promoting positive mental health, counselling is recognised as an important early intervention and preventive strategy to reduce pupils' stress levels

Types of counselling

Counselling can take a number of forms but increasingly popular is 'brief counselling' as it fits in with the time constraints of school-based intervention and is aimed at 'enabling' the pupil: a 'quick fix' rather than the deeper processes of reconstruction that is the focus of psychodynamic therapy. Research has shown that in some cases two or three sessions can lead to improvements for specific pupils, but if the aim is to change both behaviour and emotional responses, then more sessions will be required.

Finding the right type of person to provide the service is not easy as often both students and staff will be somewhat sceptical and suspicious of 'shrinks' and it can be a difficult process for pupils who struggle to develop relationships in any case. In addition, some of the other issues that will need to be addressed will include:

- provision of an environment that allows pupils to feel secure enough to expose their feelings
- constraints of timetable
- counselling aims and techniques that are in keeping with the school ethos
- resources for counselling
- planning and sustaining counselling programmes
- counselling styles that respond to individual pupil needs.

In practice, as it becomes more obvious that the results of counselling are having a positive effect on changing the behaviour and attitude of specific children, it has been my experience that both students and staff increasingly understand its value to the school community.

> Coaching focuses on improving the learning outcomes for all by providing greater focus and awareness of choice. It concentrates on the stage each pupil is at today and encourages shared responsibility to achieve where they want to be tomorrow

Coaching

For many, the terms mentoring and coaching appear to be interchangeable, but it is important to make a distinction between the two. Mentoring is usually considered to be an activity that takes place in a 1:1 situation with one person being the leader and the other the learner. In contrast, coaching is an equal partnership collaboration that suggests working alongside an individual or a group in order to achieve shared aims. Coaching supports improvement in specific skill areas and is most effective when there is a clear agenda to address that is central to the performance of the individual at the school.

Coaching can support individuals with ADHD by:

- developing knowledge and skills
- engendering trust and responsibility
- providing a supportive culture.

In a school that facilitates a coaching approach during lessons, the teachers and teaching assistants encourage verbal interaction amongst learners and use this as a springboard to encourage them to contribute observations and explore ideas further. This creates discussion, leads to greater clarity and moves learning on.

Coaching focuses on improving the learning outcomes for all by providing greater focus and awareness of choice. It concentrates on the stage each pupil is at today and encourages shared responsibility to achieve where they want to be tomorrow. It targets the attainment of all pupils as it is centred on the skills necessary for progress.

Risk-taking behaviour is encouraged, and pupils understand that incorrect responses are valued as much as correct ones for the value they bring in developing understanding. Coaching provides environments where all pupils feel secure and able to partake in discussion, knowing that their views are valued.

Skills within staff that underpin coaching and need to be supported include:

- communication and interpersonal skills
- creative thinking
- active listening
- reflective and open questioning
- facilitating confidence in others and self to make mistakes and seeing these as learning opportunities
- promoting motivation to achieve aims
- being comfortable with ambiguity and disagreement.

Coaching techniques can only be successful if seen as part of a strategic intervention that aims to increase the success of all, rather than a way of supporting an individual's needs. It requires the support of the whole organisation and may require a significant amount of preparation work to ensure that skills and attitudes are conducive to its application. Coaching requires trust and this suggests that relationships are paramount to its success. It also requires a considerable investment in time allocation to provide training, implementation and opportunities for reflection and evaluation.

Diet

Diet is obviously important to us all, not only for physical health, but also for optimal mental development and functioning. Nutrition can affect one's mood, behaviour and capacity to learn – at home, at school or in the workplace. The importance of diet can be overstated, however. For many years, diet has been reported in the media as a major factor in ADHD symptoms but most experts agree that only in a very small number of cases are children with ADHD affected by diet in a direct and obvious way.

Having said this, healthy eating with a good variety of nutritional food which provides a constant blood sugar level throughout the day, will be beneficial for all pupils. Where children live in a chaotic home, perhaps with one or other parent also having a degree of ADHD, they may not be provided with a particularly nourishing breakfast or lunchbox and this can only exacerbate their difficulties.

'Healthy eating' is on the agenda in most schools, with various celebrity chefs contributing to better school meals and a greater understanding of nutrition. It can be useful, however, to provide some additional guidance for children with ADHD and their parents, about what constitutes a balanced diet. Some supervision in the dining hall may also be valuable: schools may be providing a healthy choice at lunchtimes for example, but children don't necessarily reject what they like for what is 'good for them'!

> Scientific research on ADHD diets is limited and results are mixed. Many health experts, however, do believe that diet may play a role in relieving ADHD symptoms

Fatty acids and fish oils

Much of the research conducted into the relationship between nutrition and learning difficulties has focused on deficiencies in fatty acids. Dr Alex Richardson, Senior Research Fellow at Mansfield College & University Lab. of Physiology, Oxford University reports: *'Scientific evidence suggests that imbalances or deficiencies of certain highly unsaturated fatty acids (HUFA) may contribute to a range of behavioural and learning difficulties including ADHD, Dyslexia, Dyspraxia, and Autistic Spectrum Disorders'*.

These omega-3 and omega-6 fatty acids are found in fish and seafood, some nuts and seeds and green leafy vegetables. They are absolutely essential for normal brain development and function, but are often lacking from modern diets (especially children's). Everyone needs adequate dietary supplies of these HUFA for mental and physical health, but research shows that some people may need higher levels in their diet than others.

Individual differences in metabolism that would lead to an increase in dietary requirements include:

* difficulties in the conversion of simple essential fatty acids (EFA) into the more complex HUFA that the brain needs, i.e. DGLA and AA (omega-6), and EPA and DHA (omega-3)
* unusually rapid breakdown and loss of these HUFA
* difficulties in recycling, transporting or incorporating HUFA into cell membranes.

There is some evidence for each of these factors in children with ADHD, Dyslexia, Dyspraxia, and Autism (conditions which often overlap) and food supplements of HUFA may therefore help in the management of these conditions. Over-the-counter dietary supplements such as 'Efalex' and 'EyeQ' contain fish oils and are marketed as an effective way 'to improve brain function'. In the United States, these have been marketed to treat ADHD but at the present time this marketing campaign has had to be withdrawn due to inconclusive evidence. There are a number of studies ongoing but, currently, the balanced view appears to be that such supplements may provide some improvement in brain functioning but not to the same degree as established treatments such as stimulants. (When given with stimulants there may be an additive effect of making fits more likely in a susceptible child.)

> One area that is without dispute in terms of behaviour and learning is the benefit of hydration

Water

One area that is without dispute in terms of behaviour and learning is the benefit of hydration. Mental performance can fall by 10% when children are thirsty and it will also add to tiredness, headaches and irritability for all children and therefore is particularly important for children with ADHD who will have a lower threshold for all of these issues. Frequent, small intakes of water are better for learning than limiting drinks to breaks and lunchtimes, ideally with children needing to drink eight glasses of water during the day.

Scientific research on ADHD diets is limited and results are mixed. Many health experts, however, do believe that diet may play a role in relieving ADHD symptoms. Brain researcher and ADHD expert Daniel Amen, MD, recommends these ADHD diet suggestions:

- **Eat a high-protein diet,** including beans, cheese, eggs, meat, and nuts. Add protein foods in the morning and for after-school snacks, to improve concentration and possibly increase the time for medication to work.
- **Eat fewer simple carbohydrates,** such as candy, corn syrup, honey, sugar, products made from white flour, white rice, and potatoes without the skins.

> Children with ADHD who exercised performed better on tests of attention, and had less impulsivity than those who did not exercise

- **Eat more complex carbohydrates,** such as vegetables and some fruits (including oranges, tangerines, pears, grapefruit, apples, and kiwi). Eating complex carbohydrates at night may aid sleep.
- **Eat more Omega-3 fatty acids,** such as those found in tuna, salmon, other cold-water white fish, walnuts, Brazil nuts, and olive and canola oil. Omega-3 fatty acids are also available in supplement form.

Exercise

> Exercise should be one part of a well-rounded ADHD treatment plan

Exercise isn't just good for toning muscles as it is extremely important to keep the brain in shape, too. Exercise helps the brain release dopamine which can support attention and concentration. As stimulant medicines used to treat ADHD work by increasing the amount of dopamine, it is important to use a number of supporting options to facilitate this process.

In studies published in the *Archives of Clinical Neuropsychology* and *Attention Deficit Hyperactivity Disorder*, children with ADHD who exercised performed better on tests of attention, and had less impulsivity than those who did not exercise. Researchers think exercise works on children's brains in several ways:

- **Blood flow.** Exercise increases blood flow to the brain. Children with ADHD may have less blood flow to the parts of their brain responsible for thinking, planning, emotions, behaviour.
- **Blood vessels.** Exercise improves blood vessels and brain structure. This helps with thinking ability as the increased blood blow will allow greater brain function.
- **Brain activity.** Exercise increases activity in parts of the brain related to behaviour and attention.

> . . . getting outside and spending time in the open air can 'calm the storm' in some children with ADHD

The type of exercise offered by many schools in 'Wake and shake' sessions is an excellent way of 'getting the blood pumping', and having fun. There is a downside however to taking part in exercise as part of team games, in that many children with ADHD struggle with fine and gross motor skills so they do not excel in competitive activities and may also have difficulties in the social interactions required. This can be yet another area where they do not succeed.

The upside of course, is that perseverance can pay massive dividends; regular participation and practice in sports can have the added benefits of improving skills in both of these areas. Olympic gold medallist, Michael Phelps was diagnosed as ADHD as a child having been seen as disruptive in class but found swimming to be his outlet with regards to modifying his behaviour and self-esteem.

He has also turned out to be rather good at it! It is interesting though to note that when asked why he chose swimming he said:

'They gave me four walls and lanes I could go up and down.'

The inference is that 'if you give me the structure I will give you the performance'.

Further reading:

- Slideshow: ADHD in Children
- ADHD Health Check – Assess Your Treatment Options
- ADHD Traits in Boys and Girls
- Behavioural Techniques for Children ADHD
- Stimulant Drugs to Treat ADHD
- Drug-Free Behavioural Therapy for ADHD
- ADHD Video
- See All ADHD Therapies Topics

Beyond helping to address ADHD symptoms, there are many other reasons, of course, to get children to exercise. Engaging in regular fitness activities can help children:

- stay at a healthy weight
- keep blood pressure and cholesterol levels in a normal range
- reduce risk of diabetes
- improve self-confidence and self-esteem.

Health experts recommend that children should get at least 60 minutes of moderate to intense exercise every day. How they get that exercise (bike riding, swimming, running, soccer, dancing) doesn't really matter. There is also evidence that getting outside and spending time in the open air can 'calm the storm' in some children with ADHD. In conversation with parents and carers, teachers and SENCOs may be able to encourage them to walk or cycle to school with their child rather than travel by car, and to be mindful that the benefits outlined above suggest that exercise should be part of any well-rounded ADHD treatment plan.

Speech and language therapy

A significant number of children with ADHD experience speech and language difficulties. Speech and language therapists (SLT) need to be aware of this and the resulting additional frustration such difficulties can cause (in addition that is, to other ADHD symptoms). Common problems include:

- delayed speech development
- poor articulation (unclear speech)
- weak sequencing – sometimes an inability to finish sentences
- stuttering and stammering.

Semantic pragmatic disorder is also more common in children with ADHD, but may be harder to detect. This means that the child has difficulty in processing all the information from a situation, and responding appropriately, especially when unfamiliar subtleties of language are involved.

> Semantic pragmatic disorder is more common in children with ADHD . . . the child has difficulty in processing all the information from a situation, and responding appropriately

These language difficulties can have a significant negative effect on a child's self-esteem and willingness/ability to socialise. It's important therefore, to involve a speech and language therapist at as early a stage as possible, to develop an appropriate intervention programme and contribute to a well-balanced education, health and care plan.

In summary, helping a child to manage ADHD involves exploring a range of approaches and interventions to find a successful 'recipe'. SENCOs and teachers can help parents to consider the various options and take an active part in evaluating their impact on the child.

Chapter 8

How can teachers work with parents of children with ADHD?

Effective and proactive relationships between parents and schools will usually be vital in achieving successful outcomes for children with ADHD. It's important for teachers and SENCOs to recognise:

- the impact of the family on the child, and
- the impact of a child with ADHD on his/her family.

The actual amount of time that a pupil spends at school is very small compared with the amount of time spent at home. Parents therefore have a huge part to play in managing the child's behaviour and helping him/her to overcome difficulties. This is often a full-time job for those involved: it can be exhausting and demoralising, and a little bit of understanding from professionals (who have only to cope with the child for a few hours each day of the school week) can go a long way to establishing positive relationships between school and home. It's also important to consider the possibility of unrecognised parental ADHD and ODD when discussing the family's capacity to manage their child.

> Looking after a child with ADHD is often a full-time job for parents: it can be exhausting and demoralising, and a little bit of understanding from professionals can go a long way to establishing positive relationships between school and home

Research shows that children with ADHD often behave better for their fathers, but despite their potentially positive influence, some dads find it very difficult to cope. They may react in a number of negative ways such as being overtly aggressive with the child, avoiding going home until the child is asleep or taking sides with the child against the mother in conflicts. As a result, it is not uncommon for parents of ADHD children to experience conflict with each other. The father blames the mother for not keeping the child under control and the mother explains that nothing she does seems to work . . . This is obviously not true of all fathers, some of whom will do a fantastic job, but there is no doubt that children with ADHD can place a huge burden on family relationships especially if they also have ODD. Conflict between parents and between parents and child can, and will, have ramifications for behaviour in school.

> Research shows that children with ADHD often behave better for their fathers, but some dads find it very difficult to cope

How to manage children at home is a common question for SENCOs, and some parents of children with ADHD will try to apportion blame for any problems to teachers at the school. It will often be down to the SENCO to prevent a 'them and us' situation developing and to establish some consistency of approach between home and school. Frequent telephone/text contact, parent–teacher conferences and, possibly, daily report cards can be useful in preventing misunderstandings between school and family and ensure that any attempted manipulation of the situation by a specific child can be headed off. Remember to contact parents when there is good news as well as when there is a problem. Positive feedback about a child's progress, completing a good piece of work, helping another child or simply getting through the day without being in trouble can mean a great deal to parents.

Parenting programmes

> Most programmes combine offering practical behaviour management strategies and psycho-educational training to help parents understand their child's needs

Parents might initially feel defensive when offered the opportunity to attend a parenting programme. They may feel it represents a criticism of their own efforts and judges them as 'failing' parents. It is important, then, for teachers and SENCOs to reassure them: rearing children is never easy, and a child with ADHD poses a number of additional challenges which anyone might struggle with.

A number of parenting programmes are available and SENCOs can play a significant role in helping families to consider which might be best suited to a) the age and stage of the child and b) their own parenting 'style'. Most programmes combine offering practical behaviour management strategies and psycho-educational training to help parents understand their child's needs more effectively.

ADDISS (the UK national ADHD parents association) has outlined these options:

- Triple P (Positive Parenting Programme). A 12-week intensive course used mostly for parents of children aged from 10 into their teens
- The New Forest Parenting Programme. A 12-week course which is delivered both in groups and in the home in a one-to-one setting mostly for parents of pre-schoolers but also useful for older children.
- The Incredible Years – Webster Stratton. A 12-week course of two hours per week for children aged 3–10 years. Useful for developmental issues, changes in the family and parental mental health problems.
- 1-2-3 Magic. 3–5 week course of up 3 hours per person. Tackles difficult behaviour first then moves onto building family relationships.
- The Parent Factor in ADHD. An 8-week course of 2 hours per session, teaching parents about ADHD and all aspects of advocating for their child.
- ADHD Parent Empowerment and Skills. Developed and delivered in Lancashire.
- Training (PEST) by ADHD Northwest. A 12-week programme delivering skills to parents to help tackle all the difficulties ADHD presents to families.

These various programmes use a mixture of techniques, including role-play and group therapy. Overall, their success depends largely on the quality of the professionals involved and the openness of all parties to accept, consider and respond to objective advice. In many cases, the parents themselves will need a great deal of support and some of the essential elements of good parental training are listed below:

- family education about ADHD/ADD
- how to maximise the positive impact of medication
- developing problem-solving skills
- improving communication skills
- restoration of parental control
- reframing/restructuring
- tension reduction
- individual psychotherapy where a need is indicated.

An important benefit of attending such programmes is the opportunity to talk and listen to other parents in similar situations. Just knowing that someone else has similar experiences and worries can be a comfort. Parents can share concerns and frustrations in a sympathetic environment, support each other emotionally and pick up useful ideas and strategies which have been tried and tested by other families.

> Just knowing that someone else has similar experiences and worries can be a comfort

Home–school collaboration

A key issue for all schools is to develop positive partnerships with parents in order to provide a two-way flow of information, knowledge and expertise and this is especially important for families with children and adolescents who have ADHD. Common features of effective practice in partnership include the following:

- School staff showing respect for the role of parents in their child's education: recognising and acknowledging the part they play in teaching values and shaping behaviour
- Encouragement for parents to actively support their child's education
- Staff who listen to parents' accounts of their children's development and take action to address concerns they may have
- Ensuring that parents feel welcome, valued and necessary through a range of different opportunities for collaboration between children, parents and practitioners
- Keeping parents informed about the curriculum through brochures, displays and videos, which are made available in the parents' home language
- Regular opportunities to talk with staff and record information about progress and achievements
- Relevant school-learning opportunities being shared with home, and home experiences being valued and used to promote learning.

In some cases, parents will turn to the school and often the SENCO for advice about what they should be doing at home. This can be difficult to avoid, but care should be taken as difficulties can arise if strategies you suggest backfire. The best way to handle this is to direct parents toward the large amount of home management material available from ADDISS.

Having said this, you may have some materials available for lending to families or you may want to construct some home management checklists which you could hand out. An example of an effective home management checklist is provided in BOX 8a. You may also feel able to help them in identifying 'flashpoints' during the day when youngsters with ADHD, especially if they also have ODD, may be particularly challenging. Anticipating problems and working out strategies to deal with them can be hugely reassuring to parents.

> Parents can share concerns and frustrations in a sympathetic environment, support each other emotionally and pick up useful ideas and strategies which have been tried and tested by other families

Identifying problem times

On waking: the dawn of a new day with its forthcoming trials and tribulations can be a less-than-exciting prospect to youngsters with ADHD, especially if the previous day was fraught. They are often at their worst first thing in the morning and resistant to any form of cooperation and social behaviour. Parents can help by establishing a routine and not insisting on conversation or asking questions about the day ahead; allowing the child to eat quietly, even alone, may help to ease him

BOX 8a Suggestions for home management of children with ADHD

Be firm. Establish clear ground rules and stick to them. As the child improves in judgement, give him or her more leeway.

Avoid overwhelming the child with small, time-consuming decisions; for example, what dress to wear, what shirt, etc. If he or she dawdles and shows indecision, then make these decisions for him or her.

Consider the child's opinion whenever possible; for example, to go or not to go to Nathan's birthday party, to go to the cinema with a friend, etc. If there is no real reason to deny the child, then allow him the option of 'yes' or 'no'. However, many children with attention problems will need time to picture the situation and think it through before deciding.

Accept the absentmindedness demonstrated by most children with attention problems. These youngsters need to be reminded again and again but without the irritating 'I've told you a million times'. Try to avoid escalations of irritation when directions or reminders need to be given over and over. When you have to repeat a direction, say it each time as though it were the first time. These children are not being wilful and stubborn when they can't remember; they just can't keep the many things we expect them to remember at the forefront of their minds.

Encourage tidiness as an aid to good organisation. Note where you see him or her put his books, kit etc. Check later if the objects are still there; give a calm reminder if necessary, to put it away properly.

Be alert to the child's lapses in concentration in regard to using tools and kitchen utensils safely.

Use short lists of tasks to help a child remember. A list is impersonal and reduces irritations; the child will gain satisfaction as he checks off tasks completed.

Use simple language and short instructions. Youngsters with ADHD can seem to 'never hear' or to ignore parents' directions, requests and commands. Often, these children do not process multiple requests quickly or accurately so it helps if parents first make sure they have the child's attention before making a request. After you've stated your wish in simple, clear, one-concept commands, ask the child to repeat what was said. Speaking at a slower rate of speed is often helpful too.

Be patient. Since many children are disorganised, they may sometimes have difficulty relating an event in proper sequence. You may need to quietly ask 'who, what, where, and when' questions to get the necessary information. A calm, uncritical and non-irritable manner should be the rule.

Teach the child to take turns. A common characteristic of many children is their difficulty in waiting their turn e.g., in playing a game or when participating in a conversation. Some interruptions when adults are talking may be allowed, but having permitted some infractions of good manners, parents should correct the child sharply if he persists in interrupting.

Insist on appropriate behaviour in public. Do not permit the child to be unduly loud in a public place. Do something about it quickly, then and there, even if it is embarrassing for all concerned. Saying, 'Just wait till I get you home', will not help the child and will only make parents feel frustrated.

Establish good routines: a regular time for meals, homework, TV, getting up and going to bed. Each family should find the schedule that suits it best.

Be a mum (or dad) rather than a teacher. In the majority of instances, parents should not try to tutor their own child. It is helpful to listen to developing readers and to provide 'secretarial' support, for instance reading out challenging text for a youngster to make sure he understands it properly. But trying to 'teach' a child for example, the concepts of mathematics, is usually unsuccessful and can result in strained relationships.

or her into the day. Preparation of the school bag and any sports kit, completed homework etc, the night before, is often a good idea.

On coming home from school: any bad experiences and frustrations that have been 'bottled-up' at school may result in an 'explosion' of bad behaviour in the less rigid environment of home. He or she may feel exhausted. Routine may help – if the youngster sees home as a 'safe-haven', he or she may respond well to the opportunity to relax in front of the TV or games console for a while, and feel more in control. Try to avoid interrogation about his or her day.

Parties and eating out: parents may need to accompany children to friends' parties to manage their behaviour and avoid disruption of the celebrations; consider leaving early, or arriving late, if you think it will help: host parents will understand . . . and appreciate your efforts. Meal times anywhere can be difficult, especially if a child's medication suppresses his or her appetite, and/or if there is oppositional behaviour. Eating separately at home may be a good idea some of the time; in restaurants, parents should consider buffet options where there is no waiting, and take along something to occupy the youngster if he or she finishes eating before everyone else.

Bedtime: sleep can be a problem for children with ADHD, sometimes exacerbated by medication. Getting enough rest is important however, as for all children, so parents need to establish a definite routine and be firm about him or her staying in bed after a certain time; children can be allowed to read until they feel sleepy but parents may need to enforce a 'lights out' rule.

Family outings: children with ADHD can find new experiences and unfamiliar places a challenge. Good preparation can help, with parents explaining the overall plan for the day, timings etc. It's important to set out clear expectations of behaviour for the trip, perhaps with a particular incentive offered. Providing a focus for the child can help: e.g. taking photographs to record the outing, finding out about a specific topic (e.g. a particular animal at the zoo) or helping to navigate around the theme park.

> Teachers and SENCOs can steer parents in the appropriate use of rewards and sanctions so that there is consistency between home and school and maximum impact is achieved

Rewards and sanctions

Teachers and SENCOs can steer parents in the appropriate use of rewards and sanctions so that there is consistency between home and school and maximum impact is achieved. Of course, it's much easier for parents to motivate children with the huge range of rewards within their gift; teachers have to do their best with praise, house points and 'golden time'! But the simple message that rewards are more powerful than punishment, is one that parents may need to hear and take to heart. The next step is to establish a hierarchy of rewards so that parents avoid 'over-promising', are unable to deliver and therefore lose credibility with the child. A points system can be used in the home in much the same way as in school: collect three points for a chocolate bar; ten points for a visit to the park/swimming pool/skate-board yard; twenty points for new trainers. Parents must understand the importance of keeping their word in respect of giving rewards.

When the child is misbehaving or not cooperating, parents may use the 'yellow card' warning, explaining clear consequences, then use a 'countdown' (5, 4, 3, 2, 1) to elicit the required response. If this is not forthcoming, they **must** respond accordingly; allowing the child to escape consequences will effectively reinforce undesirable behaviour, but also make him or her feel insecure. A 'time out' approach can be just as effective at home as at school. Where sanctions have to be applied (and again, some parents will benefit from a discussion about this), golden rules include:

- 'the punishment should fit the crime', and be appropriate for the age of the child
- punish the behaviour and not the child: avoid 'you are a very naughty boy' and say instead, 'that was a naughty/careless/mean thing to do'

> Schools should also be aware of some of the possible effects on children of having a sibling with ADHD, and work with parents to minimise any negative impact

- apply the sanction immediately after the offence so that there is a clear association between the undesirable behaviour and the punishment
- avoid physical punishment
- explain to the child exactly what he or she has done wrong and why you are punishing him or her
- keep the punishment short
- the sanction must clear the air; an apology may be appropriate, but in any case, the parent should not continue to accuse or grumble.

Siblings

Parents should be encouraged to help other members of the family to recognise and understand the youngster's differences. Grandparents and members of the extended family will be more likely to tolerate impulsive, loud, forgetful, clumsy behaviour if they know the reasons for a child's behaviour and understand that it is not 'wilful disobedience'. This is especially important for siblings as their patience with their brother or sister who has ADHD will be of great assistance to the child. They may also have to accept that there are different parental expectations within the family; lower standards of behaviour may be tolerated where the brother with ADHD is concerned and this can be extremely hard to digest. Guiding parents on how to manage this situation will be invaluable, with suggestions that might include:

- making sure that siblings understand ADHD
- avoiding criticism of the child with ADHD in front of siblings
- acknowledging a sibling's cooperation and understanding – perhaps in a 'we're in this together' sort of way
- taking care to give time and attention to siblings – ensuring that the child with ADHD does not sap all parental energy and patience at the expense of brothers and sisters (where single parents struggle with this, they should try to involve other family members, friends and/or understanding neighbours)
- rewarding siblings for their support
- ensuring that siblings have opportunities for friends to visit (this may involve the child with ADHD being somewhere else); completing homework; pursuing their own interests.

Schools should also be aware of some of the possible effects on children of having a sibling with ADHD, and work with parents to minimise any negative impact. For example, strained relationships in the home can make for a tense atmosphere which is not conducive to siblings' emotional well-being. Lack of sleep, having to 'compensate' for a brother's difficulties in some way, and feeling perhaps 'invisible' for most of the time, are all commonly cited as the 'downside' of having a sibling with ADHD.

Finally and most importantly, parents themselves need to come to terms with their child's deficits and strengths. It will be important to recognise that the child has a handicap with which he or she will often need help, for many years. Parents and family members need to be realistic in what they expect, and in the goals they set for their child with ADHD.

Chapter 9

How can transitions be made less problematic?

Transitions can present challenges for any child or teenager: familiar surroundings, faces and routines must be left behind and new ones have to be accommodated. For the individual with ADHD the transition process can be particularly problematic. Teachers and parents need to be aware of the issues and how to support the child through a period of change, and teacher/TA training programmes should address the characteristics of effective transition management.

KS1 to KS2

Moving from a less structured, play-orientated environment to a more formalised classroom setting may both be problematic but also beneficial for children with ADHD. The early years environment may have suited the ADHD impulsive learning style, but the potential for accidents and incidents may have already led to the child with ADHD acquiring a 'reputation' amongst teachers, peers and parents of the other children. As a result, the more structured classroom environment may provide an opportunity for the application of rules, rituals and routines needed by children with ADHD.

However, most important of all and most difficult to implement, is the acceptance of peers and of the parents of peers regarding a child who may be seen as disruptive and difficult but who is essentially, just 'different'. It is likely that some degree of social exclusion has already taken place: play-dates, party and sleep-over invitations may not have been received by the child with ADHD, leading to loss of self-esteem and confidence by the individual and his family.

Wherever possible, it is advised that during PSHE and Circle Time or Circle of Friends sessions, opportunities should be taken to explore the differences of individuals within an inclusive community. Early years teachers and their assistants can also achieve a great deal by modelling appropriate responses to the child with ADHD so that other children take their lead: 'Freddie is having a difficult day today, so let's all be especially kind to him'. Encouraging children who are good role models to partner 'Freddie' on occasions will also provide him with a positive steer and protect against him becoming stigmatised.

> Wherever possible, it is advised that during PSHE and Circle Time or Circle of Friends sessions, opportunities should be taken to explore the differences of individuals within an inclusive community

Primary to secondary school transition

One of the most important decisions to be made about a child's education involves the choice of secondary school. For parents of a child with ADHD, this is especially challenging: they will look for a secondary school that can offer a level of understanding and continuity of structure similar to that provided by a successful primary school. This can be a difficult quest. Time and time again, hopes and aspirations of parents have been dashed by the huge differences that exist between primary and secondary settings. They need to be aware of what can reasonably be expected, how they can differentiate between schools and the criteria to use in making an all-important choice. The primary school SENCO has a crucial role to play in this process, ensuring that parents are well informed and able to ask appropriate questions in respect of the most relevant issues. In addition to all of the usual features of schools such as facilities, academic success, reputation etc. the parents of a child with ADHD will also be concerned with:

- the attitude of the headteacher and senior management team (SMT) with regards to SEN in general and ADHD in particular
- the role, status and expertise of the secondary school SENCO (has he/she got experience of supporting children with ADHD?)
- the school's arrangements for supporting children with ADHD during non-structured time
- how the school deals with, and helps to improve pupils' weak personal organisation
- how class work and homework is differentiated
- the school's attitude towards working with external agencies (e.g. Educational Psychologists, Health, Social Services and those involved in antisocial behaviour)
- how the school/SENCO communicates with parents
- arrangements for the child to take medication (though long-acting medication formulations can provide unbroken coverage throughout the school day).

(Thompson, Morgan and Urquhart 2003)

> What the glossy school brochure says the school can do, and what it really can do, will very much depend on the attitudes of the head teacher, SMT and governors

It's very difficult for a SENCO to predict the outcomes of transition of a specific student to a specific secondary school. What the glossy school brochure says the school can do, and what it **really** can do, will very much depend on the attitudes of the head teacher, SMT and governors regarding ADHD. Establishing good links with neighbouring schools and colleagues will provide an insight into school policies and management, however, and help to determine how flexible they can be with students with ADHD. A good indication of a school's ability to provide stability and a caring ethos is a low turnover of personnel and a happy and contented staff.

Perhaps the most important of all these issues, however, is the attitude, experience and status of the secondary school SENCO and how much influence she or he exerts in relation to teaching and learning across the school, and behavioural policies. This will often determine the approach of the rest of the staff.

Questions to ask

In determining which school is most 'on the ball' in terms of being equipped to support a child with ADHD, the list of questions below could be useful. Parents can also ask if there are any children with ADHD in the current cohort and, if so, what arrangements have been made to support them.

Organisational issues

Ask whether the following will be provided:

- student planners and homework diaries (perhaps on laptops)
- laminated timetable cards
- lockers or drawers for storing personal items and PE kit
- peer support or 'buddies'

- pens/pencils/rulers if needed
- a second set of books for homework to be kept at home
- help with time management
- school information emailed to home.

Classroom practices

Ask about differentiation, intervention and equipment/approaches used:

- touch-typing training, computers, Dictaphones, predictive software and programmes such as *Units of Sound*, *Word Shark*, and *Number Shark* etc . . .
- specific teaching of 'the language' of Maths and Science
- development of fine or gross motor skills
- speech and language therapy
- team-teaching by staff and TAs.

Homework

Support mechanisms can include:

> The attitudes and behaviour of the student body will often determine the outcome for the child with ADHD, so a school ethos that is truly 'inclusive' is essential for successful transition

- reducing homework to that which is essential
- shortening assignments or awarding bonus points for doing more
- reducing writing requirements, i.e. dictation onto tape recorder or computer use
- providing a study-club where students stay at school to finish homework
- allowing parents or older siblings to be a 'secretary' for students with handwriting difficulties.

Unstructured time and informal activities

Key areas that will require some degree of contingency planning for students with ADHD will include:

- break time/lunch time
- sports sessions
- field trips
- assemblies
- end of term activities.

Without some proactive, pre-planned arrangements for the areas listed above it is unlikely that transition will be successful for students with ADHD in the secondary school environment.

Peer support and understanding

In addition it would be good to have some idea about how a secondary school helps its more traditional learners to understand the issues that their peers with SEN may have. The attitudes and behaviour of the student body will often determine the outcome for the child with ADHD, so a school ethos that is truly 'inclusive' is essential for successful transition. This acknowledgement and appreciation of 'diversity' in all its forms can be evidenced through the school's rewards and sanctions system; tutor group discussion; peer mentoring; case study material and visits from past pupils who can speak positively about how they have achieved success while coping with ADHD or other difficulties.

How can parents and teachers prepare children for transition to secondary school?

- Try to buddy up the child with a peer who will be in same class – before starting
- Assign an older Peer Mentor at the school
- Rehearse the journey to and from the school in advance
- Ensure that clear expectations are communicated (from parents, and teachers) at the beginning of the year, perhaps with a reward system in place
- Teach coping strategies
- Exchange information between parents and all professionals involved with the child (including 'what has worked for us') in advance
- Ensure regular communication between all parties.

Transition to further education or training

Moving from school into college or to the workplace is an exciting time, but for many young people, especially adolescents with ADHD, it can also be traumatic.

> The most important principle will be to direct adolescents with ADHD towards academic courses, training or apprenticeships that best fit their personalities and their abilities

Change of routine is never easy for young people who depend on structure in familiar circumstances. Having said this, the opportunities to focus on specific subjects or follow a skills-based approach to employment can work extremely well for individuals who have found school difficult, possibly boring, and who may have had negative experiences with teaching staff.

The most important principle will be to direct adolescents with ADHD towards academic courses, training or apprenticeships that best fit their personalities and their abilities. This may involve a lot of research and sifting through course requirements and descriptions – something which students with ADHD may need a lot of help in doing. The opportunity to talk through all of the possibilities, 'think aloud' and weigh up the 'pros and cons' of various routes will be invaluable. This is where a trusted and knowledgeable adult can make all the difference: the role may not be filled by a parent necessarily, but another family member, a teacher, mentor or older student.

> At post-16 ADHD is regarded by the DfE as a special learning difficulty alongside Dyslexia and Dyspraxia. Students can therefore apply for a DSA (a Disability Student Allowance) to help with both materials and other means of SEN support.
>
> https://www.gov.uk/disabled-students-allowances-dsas

Relationships

While all teenagers need supportive relationships, adolescents with ADHD are particularly in need of guidance from caring adults. The statement that 'I had someone who cared' or 'someone believed in me' is so often the comment of the successful college student with ADHD.

Positive, supportive relationships are the cornerstone of successful transition at post-16; strong emotional bonds between adults and teens provide the backdrop where failure and fears can be explored. This is where plans can be made about how to react in different situations, where motivation can be nurtured and plenty of encouragement provided. In many cases, a trusted relative or good family friend will fulfil this role but schools and colleges need to be mindful of students who are not afforded this kind of support.

Coaching and mentoring can be valuable options here and colleges/sixth forms should consider including these types of intervention in their provision for students with ADHD.

(As described in more detail on pp.41–44, Chapter 5.)

> Students with ADHD will need a great deal of understanding and support in coping with the additional freedoms that come with leaving the more structured school-based environment

FE college staff

It used to be thought that ADHD was a childhood disorder but in truth, if you are born with it you will have the symptoms throughout life. How these manifest, however, will depend to some extent on self-motivation and support rather than biological maturity alone. Young people with ADHD who make the transition to FE college or sixth form will still have particular issues and their tutors will need to be aware of them, but at the time of writing there appears very little relevant training for staff within the FE field. This makes it especially important for secondary SENCOs to liaise with colleagues and share information and good practice.

Students with ADHD will need a great deal of understanding and support in coping with the additional freedoms that come with leaving the more structured school-based environment, and particular help with:

- organisational skills
- report writing
- time management
- project-based work
- extra curricular activities (including social events)
- careers planning.

Alternative skills pathways

Though we have for some years been working on the development of a more inclusive education system, it is quite clear that specific students need a different approach to that offered by the conventional curriculum in a traditional school-like setup. The better variety and quality of vocational routes to employment are, therefore, vital pathways of development for non-traditional learners. Options for this include looking at more practical skills within the '4Cs' area, especially for teenage boys (construction, cooking, cars and computers), considering diploma courses instead of more academic GCSE/A levels, and becoming familiar with the expanding range of providers, e.g. University Technical Colleges (UTC).

BOX 9 Alternatives to university include:

Apprenticeships

College/University Technical College

Gap year/working abroad

Paid employment

School leaver schemes

Setting up a business

Work experience/voluntary work

Entry to armed forces (army, royal navy, RAF)

Emergency services (police, ambulance, fire service)

www.unisnotforme.com

ADHD and the workplace

Although having ADHD can make life difficult during school years, entry into adulthood and the world of work often brings positive change. Adults with ADD/ADHD can be seen as individuals who have high energy levels, creative thinking and good problem-solving skills as well as the ability to hyper focus on a task. The ability to think conceptually, view the entire situation and find solutions to problems that are highly advanced and ingenious can be seen as extremely advantageous.

> Much will depend on the attitude of managers and their level of understanding about ADHD: some may feel that asking for accommodations is like asking for special, 'favourable' treatment

There are, however, several ADD/ADHD traits that make the workplace a difficult and trying place. Forgetfulness, inattention to detail, poor listening, poor communication and short attention spans are some of those traits and having to ask for accommodations can make individuals feel weak and worried that they will be viewed as not being able to live up to expectations. Much will depend on the attitude of managers and their level of understanding about ADHD: some may feel that asking for accommodations is like asking for special, 'favourable' treatment and that this may disrupt the dynamics of the department, causing resentment on the part of other workers. Others will be more sympathetic and flexible, as long as ADHD is not used as an excuse for poor work performance.

Overall it is best to advise young people with ADHD to be 'up front' about the issue. Honesty and trust between employer and employee is needed so that performance reviews and promotion prospects are not adversely affected.

Practical steps to support transition to college or workplace

Although it is difficult to advise individuals with ADHD on specific study and work practices because of the range of variables, some general suggestions could be as follows:

Organisation

- Use a timer/watch with alarms and set it to vibrate or beep at certain intervals during the day. The vibration/beep should remind you to get back on task and remain focused.
- If you work with a computer on your desk, you can use your computer to set reminders. Use your email and send yourself a message on deadlines, things to do and projects to be completed.
- Use a '32 file system'. Set up manila folders, one for each day of the month and one for anything past this month. File your work under the day that you need to work on it, with reminders in upcoming days for deadlines. If your work is mostly on the computer or does not involve paperwork, write a note about what needs to be completed and place in the correct date. Anything not needed to be completed this month, write a date on the top corner of the paper and file it in 'later'. At the beginning of each month, refile the 'later' papers into the correct dates. Each morning, you should have a file containing the work that needs to be completed that day. Anything for tomorrow is off your desk and remains unseen.
- Use a PDA (personal digital assistant). This device, as with all management systems, is only as good as you want it to be. You will need to discipline yourself to use the PDA and input the data you need to keep you organised.
- Use a coach or a buddy system to have someone remind you of important dates, deadlines or other work to be completed. Establish a regular time for communicating via phone, in person or by email.
- Ask your supervisor/manager to meet briefly with you each Monday morning to review the projects and expectations for the week.

- If you work in a situation where there are numerous interruptions, keep a stack of index cards or 'sticky notes' on your desk. When interrupted, immediately write down what you were doing when interrupted, or what you intended to do next.

> Taking on extra work because you impulsively agreed to do it can be devastating

Hyperactivity

- Set your schedule to allow for time to stretch, walk around and otherwise use up some of the excess energy. Pace your time so that 'sitting' work is divided into chunks, rather than long stretches.
- Use your lunch hour to exercise. Take a walk around the building.
- Ask about completing some of your work at home so that you change your environment, decreasing your restlessness.
- If you attend meetings and can't seem to sit still and concentrate, keep a pad with you and constantly take notes on what is being said.
- Restructure your workday to complete boring and mundane tasks first.

Impulsiveness

- Taking on extra work because you impulsively agreed to do it can be devastating. Talk with your supervisor or manager and let them know that you may sometimes take on more than you are able to complete. At the moment it may sound great, but later, you realise that you have over-extended yourself. Let your manager know that you would like time to think about additional projects before giving a commitment.
- Keep your day structured to avoid impulsively moving from task to task.
- Blurting out comments and answers can sometimes happen because you fear that you will forget what you wanted to say if you wait a few minutes. Keep a small notebook with you at all times and when someone is talking, write a short note to yourself about what you want to contribute to the conversation or discussion. When they have finished talking, you will be able to add your comments, without having interrupted or spoken without thinking first.

The key principle for adolescents and adults is to make sure that a degree of discipline regarding organisation of materials and self will provide a platform for successful outcomes in their chosen field of work or study.

In summary, transitions of all sorts can pose problems for individuals with ADHD to a greater extent than for their peers. Moving to a different environment can, however, also bring new opportunities and a chance of a 'clean slate'. Careful preparation for change, with the support of a trusted adult and/or a responsible peer can achieve much in minimising anxiety and enabling the youngster to make a 'good start'.

Chapter 10

Professional development for teachers and assistants

It is every teacher's responsibility to make good provision for children with special educational needs, including those with ADHD. The SENCO plays a pivotal role in shaping and steering the sort of CPD that will equip colleagues to improve their understanding and develop expertise in this respect.

The dissemination of knowledge and skills to colleagues is essential to achieving good, consistent, 'everyday-in-every-classroom' inclusive practice. Tim Brighouse quoting American researcher Professor Judith Little, has said that four factors are visible in an outstanding school:

- teachers talking about teaching
- teachers observing each other's practice
- teachers planning, organising and evaluating their work together rather than separately, and
- teachers teaching each other.

These features are particularly applicable when we're thinking about developing high quality, whole school SEN provision. SENCOs can lead by example in stimulating conversation in the staff room about teaching and learning, sharing strategies that have actually been seen to work with children who have difficulties in concentrating and conforming to behavioural expectations.

A mixed economy of CPD activity will enable you to offer a good range of opportunities for staff (teaching and non-teaching) to develop their knowledge and skills. The list below provides ideas to consider and in this chapter you will find summary sheets for each section of the book, highlighting the main points and some key facts. These can be used as handouts, posted on the staffroom noticeboard (real or virtual) and shared with parents/carers. They provide starting points for discussion and further reading and will be particularly useful for teachers of children diagnosed with ADHD, or identified as possibly having the condition. Many of the strategies suggested will be useful in a general sense – with all kinds of learners, as is often the case with good SEN practice.

Planning CPD

Add to the list from your own ideas and repertoire and use it to plan and record activities.

Type of activity	Details: dates, focus, staff involved
Local and national exhibitions, seminars, conferences: specify how attendees will disseminate to colleagues	
Guest speakers from the LA, national support groups, neighbouring (special) schools and organisations such as nasen	

Type of activity	Details: dates, focus, staff involved
Parents of children with ADHD invited to address staff	
Coaching and mentoring partnerships amongst teachers and other professionals (e.g. SLTs)	
Information available in the staffroom ('at a glance' guide to ADHD and other conditions; journal articles etc.)	
A good practice exchange system established via the intranet	
Networking with other schools (in your cluster) to share good practice, expertise and training	
Lesson observations with a focus on inclusion and effective differentiation for children with ADHD (perhaps recorded and shared with colleagues)	
Regular, planned opportunities for talk amongst colleagues about successful strategies for managing behaviour	
Collecting and sharing feedback from pupils with ADHD – to provide useful insight into what actually works for them	

Providing professional development for colleagues is a key part of the SENCO/Inclusion manager role. Throughout this book, there has been an emphasis on sharing knowledge and understanding about ADHD amongst everyone involved with a child.

Starting a discussion

Sort the statements below into three categories: **agree, disagree, not sure.**

1. ADHD affects more boys than girls
2. Pupils with ADHD invariably have a low IQ
3. ADHD can be described as a neurobiochemical condition caused by dysfunction of specific neurotransmitters within the brain
4. ADHD is linked with a variety of sleep problems
5. A significant number of children with ADHD are excluded from school
6. Roughly 5% of the population has some form of ADHD
7. Medication can cure ADHD
8. Medication should be avoided at all costs
9. Children with ADHD will 'grow out of it' in time
10 Children diagnosed with ADHD are simply 'playing the system'
11. Firm discipline is the best way to deal with pupils who have ADHD
12. ADHD runs in families

13. A high proportion of young offenders have ADHD
14. Children with ADHD often have other kinds of difficulties that also affect their learning
15. Pupils with attention deficit are always easy to spot because they demand attention
16. Parents are to blame if their child can't sit still and listen
17. Bad behaviour should always be punished, regardless of the cause
18. Allowing pupils to have special consideration in class is asking for trouble
19. A healthy diet can combat the symptoms of ADHD
20. Teachers in mainstream schools should not be expected to teach pupils who have ADHD

1. ADHD issues

There are many issues facing parents, teachers and other professionals with regards to ADHD. Not least of these is a lack of consistent recognition that ADHD is a real condition and not, as presented by the media, an excuse for badly behaved children.

Often, poor parenting is believed to be the major cause of ADHD, alongside carbonated drinks, inappropriate diet and video and computer games.

Some teachers take the view that an ADHD 'label' is a smoke screen and the condition does not really exist.

A real problem for children with ADHD

'I just wish I didn't have it. I'd do anything not to have it. It ruins your life'

What can schools do to address the issues and support children with ADHD?

Parents list the following steps:

- Raise awareness of the ADHD condition, the issues/challenges and the positives
- Provide training for all professionals concerned
- Improve communication between parents, schools, health services and social care
- Ensure early intervention to get diagnosis and treatment as soon as possible
- Ensure consistency in services and policies, locally and nationally
- Provide better information for parents and children
- Improve resourcing: the right support in the right place

2. What is ADHD?

ADHD is a developmental disorder caused by neurological and genetic factors, and influenced by environmental factors.

What is the prevalence?

- ADHD occurs in 3–9% of school-age children and is roughly 3 times more common in boys than in girls.
- Research suggest that up to 67% of children diagnosed with ADHD continue to have symptoms in adult life.

What are the symptoms?

Inattentive

- Pays little attention to detail in schoolwork or other activities; makes careless mistakes.
- Frequently has problems in sustaining attention (e.g. staying focused in lessons, or reading a lengthy text).
- Often seems not to be listening when spoken to directly.
- Often does not follow instructions and fails to finish tasks.
- Has difficulty with organising tasks and achieving good time management.
- Avoids and dislikes tasks which demand sustained mental effort.
- Constantly loses things.
- Is easily distracted.
- Often forgetful.

Hyperactive-impulsive

- Squirms and fidgets in seat; often restless.
- Often out of seat when staying seated is required.
- Often runs around or climbs excessively in situations where this is inappropriate.
- Has difficulty playing quietly.
- Constantly 'on the go'.
- Talks excessively.
- Blurts out answers before the questions have been completed.
- Often has difficulty with turn-taking.
- Frequently interrupts or intrudes on others' conversations or games.
- Tends to act without thinking.
- Is often impatient.
- Is uncomfortable doing things slowly and systematically.
- Finds it difficult to resist temptation.

3. How can we manage ADHD behaviour?

Be 'firm and fair'.

'Consistency' and 'regretting the punishment' are the two essential keys to success.

- Refer to rules, rights and responsibilities regularly
- Be consistent
- Be calm but assertive
- Use appropriate body language
- Use non-verbal responses to low-level nuisance
- Selectively ignore inappropriate behaviour
- Remove nuisance items
- Provide calming manipulatives/concentrators
- Allow for 'escape valve' outlets
- Use time out options
- Actively reinforce good behaviour
- Provide help over 'hurdles'
- Get parents onside
- Get peers onside
- Reward success
- Use a sliding scale of sanctions
- Use target setting to help children manage their behaviour

4. How can we help non-traditional learners?

Be consistent with the overall structure, while remaining flexible on minor misdemeanours.

Key strategies

- Seat the student near to the teacher with his/her back to the rest of the class to keep other students out of view
- Provide good role models: facilitate peer tutoring, mentoring and co-operative learning
- Avoid distracting stimuli. Place the learners away from heaters/air conditioners, doors or windows, high traffic areas, computers
- Minimise changes in schedule, physical relocation, disruptions; give plenty of warning when changes are about to occur
- Create a 'stimuli reduced area' for students to access
- Maintain eye contact with student during verbal instruction; avoid multiple commands/requests
- Make directions clear and concise. Be consistent with daily instructions and expectations
- Give one task at a time and monitor frequently
- Make sure the student understands before beginning the task; repeat explanation in a calm, positive manner, if needed
- Help the child to feel comfortable with seeking assistance (most learners with ADHD won't ask); gradually reduce assistance and encourage independence
- Use a day-book: make sure the student writes down assignments and both parents/teachers sign daily for homework tasks
- Modify assignments as necessary; allow extra time when appropriate
- Make sure you are testing knowledge and understanding not merely attention span.

5. Whole school approaches

ADHD can be successfully managed in schools when appropriate systems and strategies are understood and employed by all staff.

Structure allows children and young people to feel safe and creates security in their lives by developing clear boundaries and expectations.

How do school systems communicate and uphold clear boundaries and expectations, and how do you as a practitioner, follow through in the classroom?

Flexibility involves adapting to a range of different circumstances and needs. It complements the structure in children's lives and allows freedom, opportunity and fun for all involved. Effective flexibility requires an appreciation of different people and cultures and an understanding that fairness is not giving everyone the same, but giving people what they need.

How can flexibility work in practice? Can you give an example of how you have adapted in some way to meet the needs of an individual learner?

Rapport, Relationships and Role models are the means of selling, supporting and sustaining the long-term success of a structured yet flexible approach.

- Rapport: teachers and TAs who can 'connect' with the child who has ADHD will have a much better chance of 'getting through to him': it's worth investing time in finding out what interests and motivates him
- Relationships: use positive comments to build a good relationship with the pupil and avoid the situation where most (or all) interaction is negative
- Role models: teachers should be positive role models themselves and also introduce pupils to appropriate role models amongst older students, alumni and successful people from the world of sport, business, science etc.

How have you used role models with pupils to motivate and inspire them?

How does medication help?

Appropriate medication combined with counselling and support can be extremely effective in countering the negative effects of ADHD. SENCOs and teachers can support parents in their decisions about medication, and when medication is prescribed, teachers should be vigilant in observing and reporting any side-effects.

How does medication work?

Different kinds of medication work on the chemical messengers in the brain to regulate the child's behaviour.

> 'Medication is employed not as a chemical cosh to sedate overactive or inattentive children but as a chemical facilitator that raises chronically low levels of activity in certain parts of the brain and so regulates the message carrying process.'
>
> (Cooper 1995)

When should medication be used?

Only after comprehensive evaluation and in circumstances where:

* earnest attempts at non-medical interventions have proved insufficient
* the child is at risk of emotional and/or academic failure
* a child is at significant risk of harming him or herself or others.

How can teachers and SENCOs support the child on medication?

* Be observant and note any changes in behaviour
* Be discrete about the child taking medication
* Look out for side effects and be tolerant during the initial 'settling down' period.

6. Additional options for managing ADHD

There are a number of different types of interventions that can be helpful to children and young people with ADHD. Teachers need to be aware of these and able to support families in pursuing any additional approaches with their child.

Additional approaches include:

* **Cognitive-behavioural therapy:** can be particularly effective when combined with appropriate medication
* **Counselling:** enables children and young people with ADHD to gain a better understanding of themselves and their behaviour, and supports them in developing strategies for managing ADHD symptoms
* **Coaching:** supports improvement in a specific skill area and enables pupils to achieve more
* **Diet:** good nutrition is important for all children, but especially those with difficulties to be overcome. A small proportion of children with ADHD respond to particular foods/drinks in a direct way: fish oil supplements can be helpful for some
* **Exercise:** helps the brain to release dopamine which supports attention and concentration.

Which of these approaches are currently being used in school?

Could any new approaches be introduced for pupils with ADHD?

7. Working with parents

- **Respect their role** and their contribution; welcome them as partners in a supportive relationship built around the child
- **Understand their situation** as far as you can: feelings of frustration (sometimes even despair), feeling that they have somehow failed as parents; being unsure about how to handle their child
- **Introduce parents to others** who have children with ADHD, to facilitate mutual support and encouragement
- **Provide information** about ADHD/ADD, its associated behaviours and effective strategies for dealing with them (including helpful associations, programmes and support groups)
- **Share concerns and ideas:** remember to listen as well as to talk during parent–teacher meetings
- **Communicate frequently** to reassure and support parents; use texting, email, telephone, written notes to provide regular updates on the child's behaviour and achievements in addition to the usual review meetings
- **Offer a checklist of practical approaches** to try out at home and maintain encouragement for parents in sustaining their efforts
- **Pay attention to siblings** to avoid additional 'special needs' arising as a result of family stress (and adding to parents' problems as well as yours!).

8. Managing transitions

Teachers/SENCOs

- Ensure good communication between teachers, departments, SENCOs of 'old' and 'new' schools so that information about the child, and guidance on effective strategies, reaches all relevant personnel
- Enable the child to visit the new classroom/school and speak to staff before actually starting
- Explain new systems and rules thoroughly and check understanding
- Discuss expectations in the new setting and encourage the child to share any concerns
- Use role play to explore possible scenarios and model how the child should behave responsibly
- Suggest some coping strategies e.g. using a timer to break up activities into smaller 'chunks'
- Encourage positive friendships
- Support parents and suggest how they can help prepare their child.

Parents

- Help the child to make a good start by ensuring that he/she has appropriate uniform, PE kit, writing equipment etc.
- Establish a line of communication with a teacher or SENCO
- Check timetables from Day 1 and make copies to keep in the house. If there is a complicated system (e.g. an eight-day timetable) make sure you, and your child understand it
- Check out the homework timetable and 'handing-in' systems
- Get to know other parents and identify someone reliable who can be trusted to 'fill you in' on any information your child has forgotten or is confused about
- Listen to your child at the end of each day; show interest in what has happened at school and ask about 'highs and lows'.

Employees/managers

- Set out clear expectations of duties and responsibilities
- Be aware of aspects of the job which may be problematic for someone with ADHD (could these be assigned to someone else?)
- Be prepared to be flexible
- Assign another employee to act as 'mentor'
- Be frank and open with the trainee/worker, and with his/her workmates.

CAST (Child ADHD Screening Tool)

What is it?

CAST is a guide to aid teachers in identifying specific children who may be struggling in the classroom and/or socially with other children. It is not a definitive diagnostic tool but the first stage in determining the level of need of specific students who may be having difficulties due to Inattention, Hyperactivity and/or Impulsivity, which are the core symptoms of ADHD (Attention Deficit Hyperactivity Disorder).

The characteristics of ADHD included in CAST highlight a number of issues that certain children may have in school. They have been adapted from the Diagnostic and Statistical Manual of Mental Disorders, published by the American Psychiatric Association, the World Health Organisation International Classification of Diseases (ICD 10) and the NICE guidelines on ADHD.

How does it work?

As a teacher you may wish to complete this questionnaire if you have identified a child in your class who is struggling in the classroom or with his/her peers or for whom your normal teaching strategies do not appear to be working.

What happens next?

If a child scores a high level of A and Bs, it does not mean they have ADHD, as this is a screening guide not a diagnosis tool. CAST can be seen as the first stage of the referral mechanism for the school SENCO to organise a full diagnostic assessment if needed. The classroom teacher may also wish to implement some key strategies for proactive management of children with ADHD symptoms to see if they help.

References

American Psychiatric Association. Diagnostic and Statistical Manual of Psychiatric Disorders DSM-IV-TR (2009)

The WHO ICD-10 Classification of Mental and Behavioural Disorders

National Institute of Clinical Excellence. Full Guidance – Attention deficit hyperactivity disorder: Diagnosis and management of ADHD in children, young people and adults, March 2009.

CAST: Child ADHD Screening Tool

A guide for teachers to identify children who may be struggling due to Inattention, Hyperactivity and/or Impulsivity, which are the core symptoms of ADHD

Name _____ **D.O.B** _____ **Year Group** _____

Please rate each item accordingly in terms of how much it has been a problem in the last month. Please respond to each issue.

A= Frequently, B= Often, C= Occasionally, D= Never

Please tick

	A	B	C	D
1. Poor attention to detail and/or makes careless mistakes in written tasks	☐	☐	☐	☐
2. Has difficulty in sustaining attention during tasks or activities	☐	☐	☐	☐
3. Does not appear to focus or listen when spoken to directly	☐	☐	☐	☐
4. Fails to finish tasks and activities in the classroom	☐	☐	☐	☐
5. Has difficulty with organisational skills during tasks and activities	☐	☐	☐	☐
6. Appears unable to complete tasks that require sustained mental effort	☐	☐	☐	☐
7. Often loses pencils, pens or books	☐	☐	☐	☐
8. Appears to be very easily distracted	☐	☐	☐	☐
9. Is far more forgetful in comparison to peers	☐	☐	☐	☐
10. Often fidgets with hands and/or rocks on chair when seated	☐	☐	☐	☐
11. May often leave seat in the classroom without permission	☐	☐	☐	☐
12. Runs and/or climbs excessively in comparison to peers when not seated	☐	☐	☐	☐
13. Has difficulty in participating quietly in leisure activities	☐	☐	☐	☐
14. Appears to always be "on the go" or often acts as if "driven by a motor"	☐	☐	☐	☐
15. Often shouts out answers before questions have been completed	☐	☐	☐	☐
16. Has great difficulties in waiting turn in comparison to peers	☐	☐	☐	☐
17. Interrupts others (e.g. often butts into conversations or games)	☐	☐	☐	☐
18. May talk excessively in comparison to peers	☐	☐	☐	☐

Academic Performance

Reading level _____

Writing level _____

Maths level _____

Any further comments _____

_____

_____

_____

Scoring:

If a child scores twelve or more As and/or Bs then further assessment should be undertaken.

If a child scores between six and eleven As and/or Bs then further assessment should be strongly considered.

If a child scores less than six then further assessment may not be needed.

Assessing girls with ADD/ADHD

This brief questionnaire can be used as an initial screening device when assessing a girl for ADD (ADHD).

- ❐ I have trouble remembering and following my teachers' directions.
- ❐ I lose track of things like my house key or my jacket.
- ❐ I often forget to bring things to school that I need (lunch money, permission slips).
- ❐ I have difficulty completing school projects and writing assignments.
- ❐ At home, I get in a lot of arguments and upsets.
- ❐ Sometimes it feels like I am not good at anything.
- ❐ I have trouble being on time.
- ❐ It's hard for me to concentrate when other things are going on around me.
- ❐ My parents and teachers tell me I need to try harder.
- ❐ Other kids tease me about being spacey.
- ❐ I feel different from most other girls.
- ❐ My room at home is usually very messy.
- ❐ I talk a lot, even in class when I'm supposed to be quiet.

While many children and young people can occasionally demonstrate some of these behaviours, girls with ADD (ADHD) exhibit them chronically and across multiple settings, impairing their ability to function academically or socially on a daily basis.

More information about girls with ADD (ADHD), including separate age-appropriate checklists from preschool through high school can be found in *Understanding Girls with ADHD* by Kathleen Nadeau, Ph.D., Ellen Littman, Ph.D. and Patricia Quinn, M.D.

School policy for managing medicines

A policy needs to be clear and unambiguous so that it is understood by all staff, parents and children/young people themselves.

A policy should include:

- procedures for managing prescription medicines which need to be taken during the school day
- procedures for managing prescription medicines on trips and outings
- a clear statement on the roles and responsibilities of staff managing, administering or supervising the administration of medicines
- a clear statement on parental responsibilities in respect of their child's medical needs
- the need for prior written agreement from parents for any medicines to be given to a child (e.g. Form A1)
- the circumstances in which children may take any non-prescription medicines
- the school or setting policy on assisting children with long-term or complex medical needs
- policy on children carrying and taking their medicines themselves
- staff training in dealing with medical needs
- record keeping
- safe storage of medicines
- access to the school's emergency procedures
- risk assessment and management procedures.

Parental agreement for school or setting to administer medicine

The school/setting requires you to complete and sign this form, and hand it in to a member of staff before we can accept responsibility for giving your child medicine.

Name of school/setting:	
Child's name:	Group/class/form:
Name and strength of medicine:	
How much to give (*i.e. dose to be given, number of tablets/mls*)	
When to be given	
Any other instructions	
Number of tablets/quantity to be kept in school: arrangements for topping up supplies (**Note: Medicines must be in the original container as dispensed by the pharmacy**)	
Daytime phone no. of parent or adult contact:	
Name and phone no. of GP:	
Agreed review date to be initiated by *[name of member of staff]*:	

The above information is, to the best of my knowledge, accurate at the time of writing and I give consent to school/setting staff administering medicine in accordance with the school/setting policy. I will inform the school/setting immediately, in writing, if there is any change in dosage or frequency of the medication or if the medicine is stopped.

Parent's signature:
Print name:
Date:

If more than one medicine is to be given, a separate form should be completed for each one

References

Amens, D., (2011). *Increased ADHD Associated with "Western Diet"*. Available at: http://www.amenclinics. com/dr-amen/blog/2011/07/increased-adhd-associated-with-western-diet/

American Psychiatric Association (2013). *Diagnostic and statistical manual of mental disorders* (5th ed.). Arlington, VA: American Psychiatric Publishing.

ASEBA (2006). *Achenbach system of empirically based assessment*. Available at: www.aseba.org

ADDISS (2006). *School Report: Perspectives on ADHD*. Available at: http://www.addiss.co.uk/schoolreport. pdf

ADDISS (2004). *ADHD: Paying Enough Attention?: A research report investigating ADHD in the UK*. Available at: http://www.addiss.co.uk/payingenoughattention.pdf

Barkley, R. (2008). *Classroom Accommodations for Children with ADHD*. Available at: http://www. russellbarkley.org/factsheets/ADHD_School_Accommodations.pdf

Barkley, R. (2002) 'International Consensus Statement on ADHD, January 2002'. *Clinical Child and Family Psychology Review* 5(2) 89–111.

Barkley, R. (2000). Barkley's Model of ADHD: Behavioural inhibition and time awareness and management. In Hallahan, D. P., Lloyd, J. W., Kauffman, J. M., Weiss, M. P., and Martinez, E. A. (2005). *Learning Disabilities: Foundations, Characteristics, and Effective Teaching* (3rd edition). Upper Saddle River, NJ: Pearson Education.

Barkley, R. (1998). *ADHD: A Handbook for Diagnosis and Treatment*, New York, Guilford.

Cantwell, D. P., & Baker, L. (1992). ADHD with and without hyperactivity: a review and comparison of matched groups. *Journal of the American Academy of Child Psychiatry*, 31, 432–438.

Barkley, R. (1981). Home Situations and School Situations Questionnaires. Discussed in: Breen, J. and Altepeter, T. S. (1991). Factor structures of the Home Situations Questionnaire and the School Situations Questionnaire. *Journal of Pediatric Psychology*, 16(1), 59–67.

Brighouse, T. (2013). *How to raise the quality of teaching*. Available at: http://theprofessionaltutor.blogspot. co.uk/2013/12/tim-brighouse-how-to-raise-quality-of.html

Conners, C. K., Erhardt, D., and Sparrow, E. (1996). *Conners Adult ADHD Rating Scales (CAARS)*. Upper Saddle River, NJ: Pearson.

Cooper, P. (1995). *Effective Schools for Disaffected Students*, London: Routledge.

Cooper, P., & Olsen, J. (2001). *Dealing with Disruptive Students in the Classroom*, London: Kogan Page.

Cooper, P., & O'Regan, F. (2001). *Educating Children with ADHD*, London: Routledge.

Demaray, M., Elting, J., & Schaefer, K. (2003). Assessment of Attention-Deficit/Hyperactivity Disorder (ADHD): A comparative evaluation of five, commonly used, published rating scales. *Psychology in the Schools, 40(4)*: 341–361.

DePaul, G. J., Power, T. J., Anastopoulos, A. D., Reid, R. McGoey, K. E., & Ikeda, M. J. (1997). 'Teacher ratings of attention deficit hyperactivity disorder symptoms: factor structure and normative data', *Psychological Assessment*, 9(4), 436–444.

Department for Education (2011). *Prevention and reduction: a review of strategies for intervening early to prevent or reduce youth crime and anti-social behaviour*. DFE-RR111. Available at: https://www.gov.uk/ government/publications/prevention-and-reduction-a-review-of-strategies-for-intervening-early-to-prevent-or-reduce-youth-crime-and-anti-social-behaviour.

Department for Education (2005). *Managing Medicines in School and Early Years settings*. DFES-1448–2005. Available at: http://webarchive.nationalarchives.gov.uk/20130401151715/https://www.education.gov.uk/ publications/standard/publicationdetail/Page1/DFES-1448-2005.

Disney, E. R., Elkins, I.J., McGue, M., & Iacono, W.G. (1999). Effects of ADHD, Conduct Disorder, and Gender on Substance Use and abuse in Adolescence. *American Journal of Psychiatry*, 156(10):1 1515–1521.

Faraone, S. V., & Doyle, A. E. (2001). The nature and heritability of attention-deficit/hyperactivity disorder. *Child Adolescent Psychiatric Clinics of North America*, (2):299–316.

Germanò, E., Gagliano, A., & Curatolo, P., (2010) Comorbidity of ADHD and Dyslexia. *Developmental Neuropsychology*. 35(5):475–93.

Herman, D.L. (1999). *Dealing with ADHD: One Woman's Story*. Excerpt available at: http://life.family education.com/add-and-adhd/parenting/51069.html?page2&detoured

Kolberg, J. & Nadeau, K. (2002). *ADD Ways to Organize Your Life*. New York and Oxon: Routledge.

Low, K. (2011). *Cognitive Behavioural Therapy and the Treatment of ADHD: Interview with Dr. J. Russell Ramsay*. Available at: http://add.about.com/od/treatmentoptions/a/Cognitive-Behavioral-Therapy-And-The-Treatment-Of-Adult-Adhd_2.htm

McCarney, S. B. (1995). *The Attention Deficit Disorders Evaluation Scale* 2nd edition (ADDES-2), Columbia, MO: Hawthorne Educational Service.

Nadeau, K.G., Littman, E. B., & Quinn, P. D. (1999). *Understanding Girls with AD/HD*. Silver Spring, MD: Advantage Books.

National Institute of Clinical Excellence (2009). *Attention deficit hyperactivity disorder: Diagnosis and Management of ADHD in Children, young people and adults*. Available at: http://publications.nice.org.uk/attention-deficit-hyperactivity-disorder-cg72

O'Regan, F. (2005). *ADHD*, London: Continuum International.

O'Regan, F. (2006). *Can't Learn, Won't Learn, Don't Care: Troubleshooting Challenging Behaviours*, London: Continuum International.

O'Regan, F. (2008). 'Engaging education. ADHD: classroom to courtroom'. Discussion of *Education, Training and Employment*. Source document. Youth Justice Board. Available at: www.adhdandjustice.co.uk/shield/engaging-education.asp

OFSTED (2011). *Multiple barriers prevent children and learners from acquiring literacy skills – Ofsted*. Available at: http://www.ofsted.gov.uk/news/multiple-barriers-prevent-children-and-learners-acquiring-literacy-skills-ofsted.

Phelan, T., (1995). *1–2-3 Magic: Effective Discipline for Children 2_12*. Chicago: Parentmagic, Inc.

Richardson, A.J. (2006). Omega-3 fatty acids in ADHD and related neurodevelopmental disorders. *International Review of Psychiatry, 18 (2):* 155–72.

Riley, D. (1999). *The Defiant Child*, New York: Taylor Trade Publishing.

Safren, S. A., Otto, M. W., Sprich, S., Winett, C. L., Wilens, T. E., & Biederman, J. J. (2005). Cognitive-behavioral therapy for ADHD in medication-treated adults with continued symptoms. *Behaviour Research and Therapy, 43(7),* 831–842.

Serna, L. A., Nielsen, E., Mattern, N., & Forness, S. (2003). 'Primary prevention in mental health for Head Start classrooms: partial replication with teachers as intervenors', *Behavioral Disorders*, 28(2), 124–129.

The National Sleep Foundation (2013). *ADHD and Sleep*. Available at: http://www.sleepfoundation.org/article/sleep-topics/adhd-and-sleep

Thompson, A.E., Morgan, C., and Urquhart, I (2003). Children with ADHD transferring secondary schools: potential difficulties and solutions. *Clinical Child Psychology and Psychiatry, 8(1): 91_103.*

Voices on Identity, Childhood, Ethics & Stimulants: Children join the debate, 2011: http://www.adhdvoices.com/adhdvideos/adhdandme.shtml (accessed June 2013).

Waslick, B., & Greenhill, L. L. 2006 'Attention-deficit/hyperactivity disorder'. In Dulcan, M. K. & Wiener, J. M. (Eds.), *Essentials of Child and Adolescent Psychiatry* (pp. 323–357). Arlington, VA: American Psychiatric Publishing.

Index

Note: significant references are **emboldened**.